Lucky Number 8

Lucky Number 8

The story of an ordinary boy sabotaged to fail, who found grace enough to succeed.

Fred Garmon, Ph.D.

ISBN: 978-1-59684-988-4

Printed by Derek Press
Cleveland, Tennessee 37312
Printed in the United States of America

Dedication

As you read this book, you'll discover I am no stranger to death and loss. Pain and grief can convey agony enough to give pause as to whether life is really worth living. But the five ladies and one little man mentioned below have forever removed such a thought.

Many things also have brought me joy and happiness during my life's journey. But none as much as the six angels that were dropped into my life from paradise's shores. My wife, my two daughters, my two granddaughters, and one grandson are truly the sunlight of my life. I cannot imagine an existence that did not include them. They are without doubt the supreme pleasure and ultimate joy of my life. My greatest ambition has been to have earned their respect and an honorable remembrance in their hearts.

The great philosopher and truth-seeker Winnie the Pooh said,

"Sometimes the smallest things take up the most room in your heart."

I'm convinced that the best kept secret of life is how great it is to have children. The joy of being a parent, and now a grandparent, the amount of love and laughter it brings into your life, together with a sense of purpose and meaning, is, for me, without doubt, my greatest delight.

I love my wife, Shirley. Her place as co-author of my life is foundational and central. None of this story would have been written without her partnership in this journey.

So there is no question about it, Dr. Pooh, these ladies and one little man take up the most room in my heart.

King Poppy
The name given to me by my granddaughters.

Contents

Foreword

"Freddie's back, Freddie's back!" I vividly remember hearing those words in the fall of 1973 as I sat in the school's cafeteria, minding my own business. Little did I know at the time just how Freddie's "being back" would impact me and the entire student body at Northwest Cabarrus High School, and eventually the entire world!

First of all, I did not even know that he had been gone, and besides that, what was so unusual about this "Freddie" that would generate such excitement, curiosity, and even fear? During the days ahead, the Holy Spirit began His supernatural work in me to open my heart to this "stranger" in our midst. It is true that the Holy Spirit WILL have His way regardless of the thoughts and intentions of man. Even with an overbearing basketball coach and a policeman father who both told me to stay away from this troublemaker, I allowed my heavenly Father to be in charge, and HE always knows best. For this, I continue to be humbled and grateful.

Proverbs 19:21 NLT
You can make many plans, but the Lord's purpose will prevail.

This book you hold in your hands has the supernatural power contained within to change, revive, and spark new life. *Lucky Number 8* is a must read for every leader, young adult struggling with identity, or just the "everyday" Christian caught up in the mundane. This book will restore power in the human spirit to fight and never give up, regardless of how the dice is tossed.

Reading these pages today, after nearly forty-five years, my spirit is touched and my mind is refreshed. God is still in the healing, restoring, and, blessing business today. I challenge you to read this book with an open mind and heart. God will show Himself to you in every chapter. I am so very thankful that God chose me to share His great love and power to this general of the faith . . . now, no longer "Freddie," but Dr. Fred Garmon, Ph.D.

I am so glad Freddie CAME BACK!

Psalm 139:16

"You saw me before I was born. Every day of my life was recorded in Your book. Every moment was laid out before a single day had passed."

My prayer is that, as you read this book, you will "come back" to Him if you have been away, and that you will "come closer" to Him if you have drifted. There is no love like HIS!

Foreword by **Carol Bennick Bost**
Author: *Unfinished Love Story*

PREFACE

Lucky Number 8

Freddie was a 9-year-old boy, the baby of eight. An accident, some might say, growing up very much like an only child. He played most every day by himself, primarily living each day in a land of imagination. But all seemed fairly normal until late one night Freddie was awakened by the sound of sirens and the reflections of bright blue and red lights throughout his house. Freddie was about to experience five of the worst months of his life—five months that would forever frame a life-shattering experience that he was too young to grasp. His 18-year-old sister died that night in his front yard from a gunshot wound to the chest. Five months later his mother died of cancer. His dad retreated into a bottle of wine to help numb the grief. His brothers and sisters retreated to their own families. And Freddie would be forced to cope and survive. Freddie was about to enter a lonely "void."

As you read this story, you'll see amazing resilience. Resilience comes from deep within us and from support outside of us. We are not born with a fixed amount of resilience. It is a muscle everyone can build. Even after the most devastating events, it is possible to grow by finding deeper meaning and gaining greater appreciation in our lives.

The number 8 has long been regarded as the luckiest number in Asian culture. Fred would learn this interesting piece of information later in life while serving in southeast Asia. In the Bible, the number 8 is the number of new beginings. The number 7 is often noted as the number of completeness—the number 8, however, is one too many; unwanted and forgotten. But being a number 8 is actually something to be proud of. According to the Bible, number 8's posess God-ordained possibilities.

Lucky Number 8 combines Fred's personal story with eye-opening research, attempting to make sense of tragedy and trying to find strength in the face of adversity. Fred opens his heart to describe the acute grief and isolation he felt and endured in the wake of his sister's and mother's deaths. Fred's story and the lessons learned can be applied to everyday struggles, allowing us to brave whatever lies ahead.

We all hope for a life without pain, without loss—"Option A." But what do you do when Option A is no longer available? Freddie had to learn how to make the most of Options B, C, and D. The truth is, we all live some multiple-choice form of Option B. This book will help us all make the most of it.

You may not have been "born" a number 8, but you know you are different. There is hope for you! There is a bright future ahead.

The first 25 or so pages offer some information that sets the stage for all that follows. But if you're eager to jump straight into the details of Freddie's story, simply skip directly to section two page 29. You can come back to those initial pages at a later time.

Introduction

Pattern and Perspective

I've always liked looking at patterns. It's like standing back and admiring the work put into a handmade quilt. A *quilt* is a multilayered cloth, traditionally composed of three layers of fiber: a woven cloth top, a layer of batting, and a woven back, combined using the technique of quilting, the process of sewing the three layers together. In the process of writing this book I've found myself feeling much like a quilter. Along the way I've found myself standing back and contemplating the different layers and tapestry of my life.

I'm now 60 years old. Age provides a certain amount of *perspective* that can only be seen from this particular vantage point. As an amateur artist, the idea of perspective intrigues me. Perspective is the art of drawing objects so as to give the right impression of their height, width, depth, and position in relation to each other when viewed from a particular point. This was my goal in writing my story and in coming up with an appropriate title—*perspective.*

Therefore, after looking back on all the patterns, layers, colors, and years of my life, my attention has continually been drawn to the unique reality of being the baby of eight children, accidental and unforeseen. My mind was drawn to the fact that I was a slow-cooking baby—born after 44 weeks--and that I endured a traumatic birth. My attention was additionally drawn to the detail that my collar bone was broken at birth and no one diagnosed it till months later. Thus, the title *Lucky Number 8.*

Read the pages that follow and you decide. Was I "lucky" or was it *something else*?

SECTION ONE

Leadership development or personal change is *not* something that someone can do *to* you.

Personal change is something that only comes from a decision of the will—*your will.*

PRIMER

The Power of Hope

My personal experience tells me that *people can change*, that we can inspire hope and empower potential[1] in the lives of those we touch during our life's journey. The Bible has long been on the side of *hope*. For instance, we read in Hebrews 11:1, 6, "Now faith is the substance of things *hoped for*, the evidence of things not seen" and "without faith it is impossible to please him."

Until recently there hasn't been much rigorous research evidence that outside aid or other vehicles can sustainably lift people out of poverty, despair, and dysfunctional lifestyles. This, however, seems to be changing. According to an article in the *New York Times* (May 21, 2015) "The Power of Hope Is Real," the article reports a vast randomized trial (*www.poverty-action.org*)—the gold standard of evidence—involving 21,000 people in six countries suggesting that certain aid programs actually give very poor families a significant boost that continues after the program ends.

Such programs contain various components, and new data shows that a *kernel of hope* can be a significant mechanism. Whether in America or Southeast Asia, families that are stressed and impoverished (even people in your family or community), trapped in cycles and whirlpools of

1 "Inspire hope, Empower Potential"—A soundbite I came up with during one of my first trips to Cambodia just after becoming the executive director of People for Care and Learning, a Humanitarian Non-Government Organization (NGO). I looked in the eyes of an old Khmer lady while riding in a van on a dirt road at the Tonlé Sap Lake (the Great Lake). The lady was sitting with her calves resting on the back of her ankles staring out into nothingness. It seemed she looked right through me. Her eyes seemed to say, *I have no hope. I had no hope yesterday, I have no hope today, and I'll have no hope tomorrow.* It was in that moment that I realized, if we were to make a difference in the lives of this poverty-stricken people then we must "inspire hope" if we were to have any chance at all in "empowering their potential." This idea still serves as a guiding principle in my life to this day.

poverty and dysfunctional behavior, can feel a hopelessness that becomes self-fulfilling.

In fact, we've been seeing a wealth of psychological research, over the past 20 or so years, showing loud and clear that psychological *vehicles* like *hope* are the mechanisms that really get us to personal change and goal achievement. Many other factors are important—factors like grit, conscientiousness, self-efficacy, optimism, passion, and inspiration. But if you can't be bothered with driving your own vehicle or leading your own life, you simply will not get anywhere.

Hope seems to tap into and ignite a quality called "action orientation." It helps a person launch directly into a major task and then discipline themselves to work steadily and single-mindedly until the task is complete. Stephen Covey referred to it as having R&I, or resourcefulness and initiative. Until hope germinates, many people seem to be trapped in a vortex known as "failure to execute." Thus, many people confuse activity with accomplishment.

Hope Theory is a name given to this important motivational idea. According to this theory, hope consists of agency and pathways. Put simply: hope involves the will to get there and figuring out different ways to get there.

Why Is *Hope* So Important?

Life is difficult. There are many obstacles, and simply having a goal is not enough. Just knowing that you need to change is not enough. In the midst of all the inevitable twists and turns of life, *Hope* allows people to approach their problems with a *mindset* and a *strategy-set* that move them forward, increasing the chances they will actually make personal change and accomplish their goals.

Biblical hope too is more than wishful thinking; it goes much further than just a feel-good emotion. According to my good friend, Pastor Tom Sterbens, biblical hope "represents the deep conviction or belief in a future event or promise, to the extent that we redirect the steps of our life to intersect it, moving us beyond our subjective, limited circumstances, toward an objective reality."

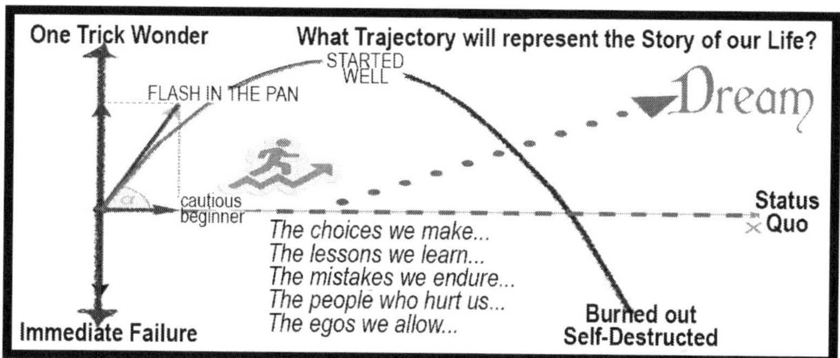

The diagram above depicts a few of the numerous pathways an individual can choose in life, from immediate failure, a flash in the pan, status quo, and living the dream. The present trajectory that represents your life will ultimately determine your life's journey. And make no mistake about it, it is *up to you*. It is *your choice*.

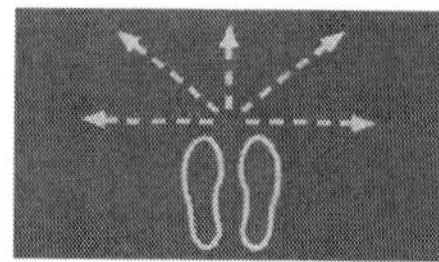

Hope, according to research, is a cognitive motivational system. Under this conceptualization, hope leads to *learning goals* that are conducive to personal growth and development. People with learning objectives become actively engaged in their learning, constantly planning strategies to meet their goals and monitoring their progress to stay on track.

Those lacking hope, according to the research, tend to adopt *mastery goals*. People with mastery goals choose easy tasks that don't offer a challenge or opportunity for growth. When these people fail, they quit. People with mastery goals act helpless and feel a lack of control over their lives. They don't believe in their ability or capacity to obtain the kind of future they want. They have *no hope*.

Science, however, seems on the side of hope. Psychologist Charles R. Snyder has come up with a way of measuring hope. The Hope Scale has now been translated into more than 20 languages and includes items (questions) relating to agency (*e.g.*, "I energetically pursue my goals") and pathways (*e.g.*, "There are lots of ways around any problem). See Appendix 1 if you'd like to take the assessment.

Both research and experience are now telling us that purely giving people a reason to hope is critically important. Helping people see that a better life is truly possible can also be self-fulfilling. As one humanitarian director stated,

> Dysfunction and poverty isn't [sic] just about money. It also involves self-esteem, hope, opportunity, and freedom. People living in cycles of dysfunction and poverty do not see that their lives can change; that they can change. Once they do see it, the light comes on.

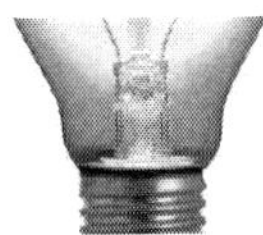

Researchers are now studying whether exposure to religion might have a similar effect—inspiring hope and improving economic outcomes. If so, Marx had the wrong drug in mind: religion would not be an opiate of the masses but an amphetamine[2]. I cannot speak for all the research concerning *hope*, but I do have a testimony involving *hope*. I can say with the biblical blind man of John 9:25, "I was blind, but now I see."

On the third Sunday of January 1974, my life seemed hopelessly messed up and out of control. That morning I knelt at a church altar in Kannapolis, North Carolina. A highway patrolman who, interestingly, knew me and my dysfunctional lifestyle, knelt beside me and whispered in my ear, "Freddie, we've tried to help you for several years with no results, but the Lord has done it in a moment's time." I had no idea what he was talking about, but time itself would validate his statement.

There may be a thousand explanations for the personal transformation that started that morning and continues to this day. All I know is that a humble prayer, simple faith, and naïve belief in Jesus Christ, along with a *kernel of hope* that seemed to appear within me from out of nowhere, ignited a seed of potential and set my life on a new trajectory.

Looking back now, 43 years from that day, my life experience tells me there is *hope*. And because I passionately believe this, I have been honored

2 A synthetic, addictive, mood-altering drug, used as a stimulant, antidepressant, pep pill, upper, pick-me-up, or happy pill.

to inspire hope literally around the world. It works! There is good news for *all*! Today does not have to be like yesterday, and tomorrow does not have to be like today. Change is possible.

It boils down to this. *Hope* is the soil needed for *potential* to grow. The *people* who come into our lives represent the sunshine and the *rain of inspiration*, *encouragement*, and *empowerment*. These wonderful people that I call *life-role leaders* are the ones who selflessly *serve* to ignite the *kernel of hope* within others.

So, it was out of my personal journey that I asked, "*Why?*" "*Why can't we inspire others to make a difference in our world?*" I have landed on a very affirming answer to this question. It is my conviction and persuasion that we can inspire hope; we can empower potential. We can use the weight of our influence and ideas to address issues concerning extreme poverty, dysfunctional living, destructive behavior, and our peculiar propensities to aim low when it comes to reaching for our true personal potential.

The Leadership Mirror

There's a lot of discussion today about leadership. Much of the conversation is cliché or vague. We talk about leaders—charismatic leaders, command and control leaders, transformational leaders, servant leaders. I now know that all leadership begins with self-leadership, and much within leadership literature and research postulates this very idea. Scripture too reminds us that all personal journeys of development and growth begin with a good look in the mirror (see James 1:23).

That *kernel of hope* I mentioned earlier ignited something powerful within me and presented me with a choice I didn't know I had. I was given the opportunity to choose a different path, a path of self-development empowered by *hope*.

Future Orientation

One of the very special gifts given to us in this life is the ability to look ahead. The capacity to imagine the future is a fundamental defining characteristic of being human. It's what the late Stephen Covey called, "Beginning with the end in mind." It is this germinated *kernel of hope* that removes the blinders and allows us to see the amazing possibilities that lie before us, the various pathways that we can choose to move forward.

G. Campbell Morgan (1863–1945), a British evangelist, preacher, and leading Bible scholar, is reported to have said, speaking of the new life and hope that come with the Christian faith, "We are all implanted with a seed of potential at the new birth."

You are not empty. There is a seed within you. That seed is the seed of greatness. It is the seed of accomplishment. That seed, given opportunity of expressing itself, enables you to achieve whatever you want to achieve in life.

I like to call this seed "potential on steroids." Potential! That which can be but has not yet come into being. That which is actually possible but is yet unrealized. That which is latent, invisible, inactive, lying hidden and undeveloped in a person.

But there is nothing more common than people who *had* potential. More often than not, we use the term *potential* in the past tense—something "had." We say, referring to so-and-so, "they had tremendous potential." The implication? The person obviously possessed idiosyncratic and distinctive characteristics that caused them to stand out. In one way or another, it was evident to others around them that they possessed the "X Factor." But their potential, whatever that could have been, was never realized. For one of a possible thousand reasons, they made a choice or choices that resulted in a product, an outcome, or a version of themselves far below the standard for which they were capable and gifted. How sad. . . .

A 2017 Gallup Poll report reveals just how pervasive such low aim is. The poll details that an alarming 70 percent of Americans are not reaching their full potential. As one writer put it, "Potential means nothing if you don't do something with it."

It boils down to the issue of leadership. Each of us must first and foremost learn to *lead our own lives*[3]. The writer in Song of Solomon 1:6 speaks to the importance of understanding this principle: "They made me keeper of the vineyards; but mine own vineyard I have not kept!"

3 "I . . . beg you to *lead a life* worthy of your calling." The Apostle Paul, one of my favorite biblical leaders, encourages self-leadership and twice in 2 Corinthians 4:1 and 16 says in spite of many hardships that he did not "lose heart." This is important given the statement found in Proverbs 4:23 (*NLT*), "Guard your heart above all else, for it determines the course of your life." As Professor Ron Heifetz said in *Leadership Without Easy Answer*, "Leadership is not for wimps."

Personal growth and development begin with self-development and self-management. The instrument of leadership is self, and mastery of the art of leadership comes from mastery of self. I believe passionately that leaders are born, then made. I believe that we can acquire a leadership toolbelt that prepares us for eventualities and opportunities that will come our way. Leadership principles like this can be learned. Acquiring skill sets, leadership, and managerial competencies is possible.

Leadership development is not, however, something that someone can do *to* you. Leadership development and personal change is something that only comes from a decision of the will—*your will.*

I've now been teaching leadership for more than 15 years; I've been using leadership principles to cultivate and inspire personal leadership improvement. Personal growth takes place when inner work is facilitated to drive healthy performance. Today I facilitate leadership workshops (LABS), knowing full well I'm not a subject matter expert on leadership; no one is. Personal change and growth is a journey, not a destination. In fact, I've learned to think of myself as a chef preparing a buffet of skills, knowledge, and leadership challenges. Those who participate in my training LABS are all at different places in their leadership journeys. They decide what to take in and how much. They get to choose. My responsibility is to keep the buffet well stocked.

I also believe that self-development is not just about stuffing a whole lot of information into an already information-overloaded brain. The quest for the best version of ourselves should never be about just filling ourselves full of facts and information. The quest for the best you possible is first an inner quest to discover who you are, what you care about, and what you value. Discovering what inspires you, what challenges you, and what encourages you.

Discover what gets you out of bed every morning. It's about changing your behavior. It's about leading out of what is already in your soul. It's about liberating the leader in you so that you can become the very best version of yourself possible. After all, who wants to come down to the end of their life and realize they left so much more on the table? As my friend Tom Sterbens song says, "There should be nothing left behind."

Clarity of Purpose

There are as many definitions concerning leadership as there are people who will read this book. But allow me to give you one of my favorite definitions from the American novelist and essayist, David Foster Wallace:

Real leaders are people who "help us overcome the limitations of our own individual laziness and selfishness and weakness and fear and get us to do better, harder things than we cannot get ourselves to do on our own."

I could say many things toward unpacking Wallace's definition. Allow me to address what I believe is principal. Accomplishing Wallace's noble task requires clarity of purpose. Clarity of purpose should be like the bullseye on your personal target of core values, ambitions, and goals. You should also choose six to nine other subordinate priorities and make sure to keep them balanced and near the center of the mark. Otherwise it is so easy to allow "things," not just bad things but good things, to crowd out the best things. It takes discipline and focus—what leadership research calls "self-management" and what Scripture calls "self-control" (see Galatians 5:22).

Think about your life, both as it is now and where you'd like it to go. Consider not just your occupation or your ministry but also your life outside these things. Consider and assess what's working, what's not, and what you might want to add or subtract.

DEFINING YOUR PURPOSE AND YOUR VOICE

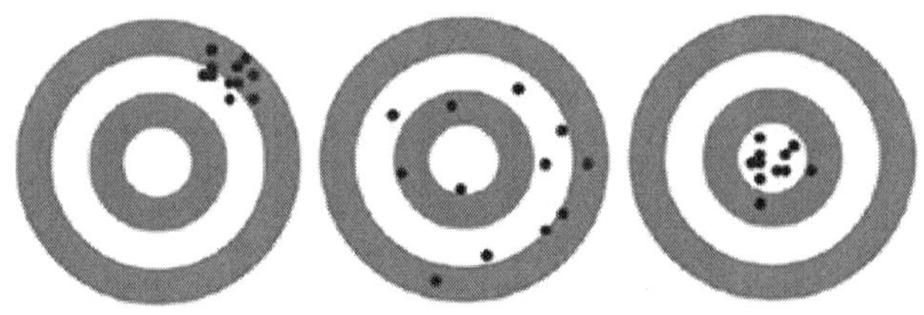

Take a few minutes to examine the graphic above. When it comes to values, purpose, and things truly important (priorities), which one of these targets best represents your life as it is right now? Be brutally honest with yourself. Next, can you tell which target would be better?

For many, the graphic above best represents their life. A great deal of energy is being inefficiently invested. A lot of activity is taking place, but nothing of real importance is being accomplished. Too many "things" are being allowed to consume valuable time, attention, and even resources. Could this be the reason seven out of 10 people are not reaching their full potential?

No wonder then that the hope provided in the Christian faith is intended to produce surprising *potential.* The hope mentioned here allegedly[4] brings with it an amazing ability to "control ourselves." And it's my persuasion that much of this control helps us to focus and pay attention. It is as if we live in a culture full of attention deficit disorder (ADD) mannequins. This is powerful stuff if we choose to take hold of it! In fact, the writer in Proverbs 25:28 says, "A man without self-control is like a city broken into and left without walls." ESV.

Tommy Propes and I have known each other since college. One day we were casually discussing leadership when he asked me what I saw to be the number-one characteristic or skill set needed by a leader? My first response was what I always say when questioned about leadership: "It depends." Then I added, "But if push comes to shove, I'd say it's what leadership literature and research refer to as 'self-management' and what the Bible calls 'self-control.' "

My friend Tommy quickly and proudly responded, "Really? My mother used to tell me, *Son, manage your spirit.*"

4 I say *allegedly* because it seems so few people actually take advantage of and learn to utilize this incredible gift and resource.

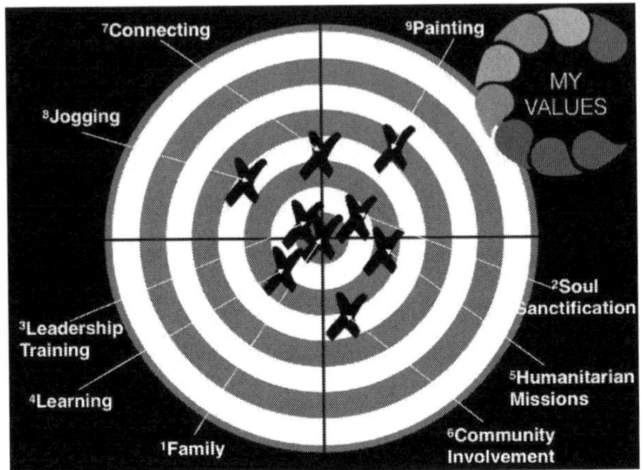

The graphic above shows an example of what I see as my personal values and priorities. Such awareness helps us to focus our energy, our calendars, and our thoughts on things that matter. This measure of awareness also helps us vet our choices, keeping our decisions in alignment with our values and goals.

These priorities are what social psychologist Milton Rokeach called "instrumental values" because they move us toward our "terminal values" or end-game goals.

In the process of reflecting on your own values, remember the words of Larry Burkett and Peter Drucker who both agree,

If you really want to know what matters most to you, take a good look at your calendar and your checkbook; they won't lie. Your priorities will jump right out at you.

Jesus put it this way in Matthew 6:21, "Where your treasure is, there your heart will be also" (NIV).

Take a moment and reflect on Appendix 2. See if you can enrich your personal journey toward becoming aware of what truly matters most to you. And remember, be honest with yourself, keeping the following two statements in your mind as you complete the survey:

Be ruthlessly honest with yourself! Go with your "gut" instinct; do not overanalyze!

A few moments of brutal self-honesty are worth a lifetime of self-deception.

The Road Less Traveled

In the next chapter, we will jump headlong into my story. But before we do, remember this:

Much of life will not challenge you to stop operating and living from your default or comfort zone settings of selfishness, pride, and fear. I hope my testimony, the story of my life-journey contained in the following pages, will challenge you to adjust those settings. I hope the pages that follow will inspire you to stop living life on automatic pilot and start *paying attention.* I hope you will be empowered to become the very best version of ***you*** that is possible.

We like to think that our present ability is the best predictor of our future possibilities. And while psychological studies show that our ability is important, it's actually the vehicles, like that of *hope*, that get us where we want and need to go. And *hope*, with all its will and ways, is one of the most important vehicles of them all.

Somewhere, sometime, the leader within each of us may get the call to step forward. Hope gives you the spark of faith and industry designed to ignite belief in yourself and your capacity to learn so that you'll be ready to lead others when that call comes. I choose to cast my vote on the side of optimism and hope.

I resonate with the following words found in Bruce Wilkinson's book *The Dreamer,* and the words serve well as a starting point for what follows. Especially for those of us who often feel like an ordinary nobody living in the familiar.

"So Ordinary, who was called a Nobody, who lived in the Land of Familiar, took a deep breath and stepped out into the unknown."

—Fred Garmon

SECTION TWO

"Brothers and sisters, think of what
you were when you were called.
Not many of you were wise by human
standards; not many were influential;
not many were of noble birth"
(1 Corinthians 1:26, *NIV*).

"Therefore, if anyone is in Christ,
the new creation has come:
The old has gone, the new is here!"
(2 Corinthians 5:17, *NIV*).

"'For I know the plans I have for you,'
declares the LORD, "plans to prosper you
and not to harm you, plans to give you hope
and a future'" (Jeremiah 29:11, *NIV*).

CHAPTER 1

Ashley's Story

Her name was Ashley. We met her in June 2017 while my wife, Shirley, and I were on vacation. We were on a six-day driving tour across Wyoming, going to South Dakota. We had started our tour in Jackson Hole, Wyoming, then driven through the Teton National Park and Yellowstone National Park. Next we took off across the state, heading for the old western town of Deadwood and the bucket-list site of Mount Rushmore.

We truly enjoyed driving across Wyoming but quickly found out why so much of the state is referred to by many as a "fly-over state."[5] We drove for hours without seeing much of anything and mentioned to each other several times, "Why in the world would anyone want to live out here?

5 *Fly Over States*—States in the middle of the United States that generally aren't destinations for travelers or tourists and are generally flown over when traveling from coast to coast. Some fly-over states include Nebraska, Oklahoma, North Dakota, South Dakota, Wyoming, New Mexico, Iowa, and Arkansas.

There is nothing here." About every hour and a half, we'd come into a little town; not much there other than a gas station and small market.

We were in the middle of nowhere headed toward Deadwood, driving through an amazing canyon of rock with a beautiful stream flowing all along the winding road and steep cliffs on both sides. We suddenly noticed an orange flag waving up and down a mile or so ahead of us as we coasted deeper into the canyon. Continuing our descent, we noticed a young lady construction worker whose job it was to stop and release traffic. She had a hand radio used to communicate with another flag person a mile away. We watched as the last car before us went ahead and we were the next car to be stopped, allowing vehicles on the other side to come through.

We slowed down and came to a stop. Shirley leaned out her window and asked the construction worker how long we would be detained. We learned that a construction crew was just around the bend ahead, pulling loose boulders from the side of the cliffs. Traffic was alternately being stopped on both sides of the construction area. We would have to wait 30 minutes, so I turned off the car and Shirley got out to stretch and talk. I sat in the car, rolled down the windows, and pulled out a book to read. It wasn't long until the conversation became much more interesting than my book. I leaned over and started listening.

Ashley was a thin pretty young woman with long blonde hair. She was dressed in worn blue jeans, construction boots, wearing a florescent yellow safety vest, t-shirt, and hard hat. We deduced from the conversation that she was probably in her late 20s.

Shirley jokingly said, "What's a pretty girl like you doing out here?" Ashley laughed and said, "Yeah, I'm having a pretty good day. The truckers are blowing their horns and yelling out their windows more than usual."

Ashley was personable and talkative and voluntarily shared personal information.

Napoleon initially stated it this way: "The role of a leader is to define reality and give hope."

My paraphrase expands the thought like this:

> How can I learn to be brutally honest with myself and see things as they truly are? How can I find foresight enough to construct a vision of my future that fuels hope? Because without hope I'll never break free from the vortex of despair. I urgently need *hope*—for it is hope that motivates me to break free from my chains and climb toward the mouth of the cave and behold the sunshine, to see reality.

It is my desire that this book does so for people like Ashley, for people like you or for someone you love, care about, or know. My expectation is that my story will spark the faith and germinate the hope that can inspire and empower people with courage to see the reality of their present situation. I hope you will find inspiration and empowerment that will enable you to pull yourself out of the vortex, out of the quicksand of dysfunction.

If I did it, you can do it. It can happen!

You can do it! Have *hope*.

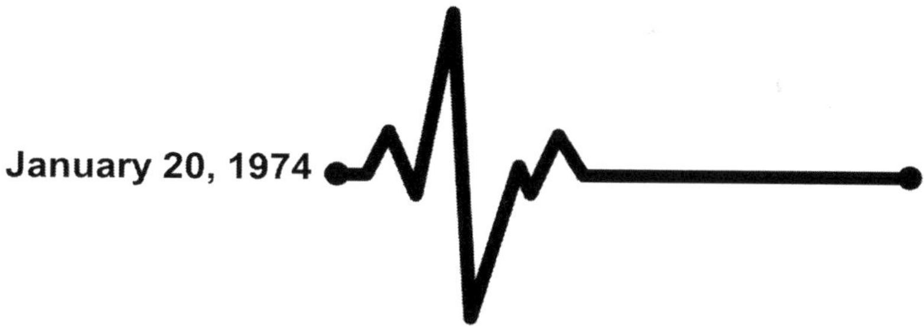

CHAPTER 2

20/20 HINDSIGHT

It has been said that "hindsight is 20/20 if you'll look" and that "life can only be understood backwards; but it must be lived forward" (Soren Kierkegaard). As I began writing this book, I was 59 years old, looking back at almost six decades of my life . . . my story, my journey. For the last two-thirds of my life, I've been living my dream, an unfolding narrative that seemed impossible considering how my story began.

Author Bruce Wilkinson wrote in his book *The Dream Giver*

The journey toward your Big Dream changes you. In fact, the journey itself is what prepares you to succeed at what you were born to do.

And until you decide to pursue *your* dream, you are never going to love your life the way you were meant to.

I could have written those words. They resonate so perfectly with my experience in life. My journey has changed me. But then, isn't that true for all of us? For good or for bad, our experiences, the deck that is dealt us, changes us. But it is what we choose that makes the difference in how the journey progresses and how the narrative unfolds. It is the dash between the dates of our life that will determine the outcome.

> What came first was the date of birth.
> And spoke the following date with tears,
> But what mattered most of all
> Was the dash between those years.[8]

It was but a simple line. It was the dash between the dates, placed there, it stood for time.

How important is that little line?

8 "The Dash," Linda Ellis, author.

As I look back, I observe several major bifurcations, several forks in the road, choices and particular events that so impacted my life journey as to change the very trajectory of my life. These experiences would cause me to alter the steps and behavior of my life to intersect with a future hope and aspiration that my particular journey would shape. I will attempt, therefore, to draw attention to such special markers, events that impacted me negatively and positively. After all, it is the totality of our lives, the aggregate, the culminating whole of our lives, that creates our story.

My personal journey informs me that *people can change*—there is *hope*, and hope is the soil needed for *potential* to grow. The people who come into our lives via life-role relationships (pastors, youth pastors, coaches, school counselors, friends, family members, teachers, professors, baristas, etc.) represent the sunshine and the rain needed for *potential* to develop, to produce the outcome of a life that makes a difference.

Context

My life started on Monday, September 9, 1957, when I was born at Mercy Hospital in Charlotte, North Carolina. Dwight D. Eisenhower was the 34th president, a five-star general in World War II, who served two terms (1953-1961) and was succeeded by John F. Kennedy. Paul Anka's song, "Diana," reached #1 that year. In addition, the first 13 years of my life would be seriously impacted by the 1954 Supreme Court Ruling that ended Segregation[9] in the United States, especially throughout the South.

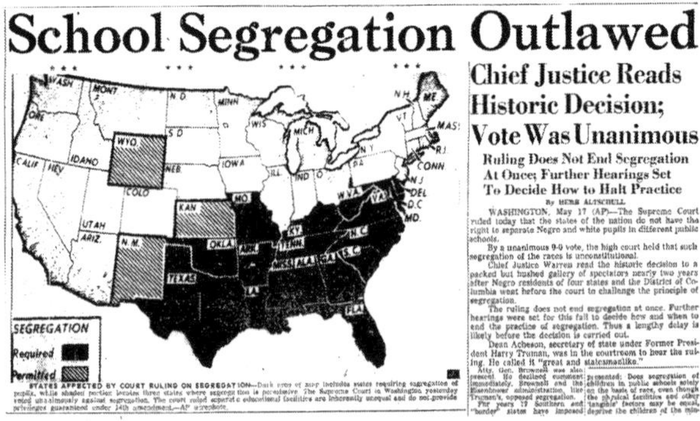

School Segregation Outlawed

STATES AFFECTED BY COURT RULING ON SEGREGATION—Dark area of map includes states requiring segregation of pupils, while shaded portion locates three states where segregation is permissive. The Supreme Court in Washington yesterday voted unanimously against segregation. The court ruled separate educational facilities are inherently unequal and do not provide privileges guaranteed under 14th amendment.—AP wirephoto.

Chief Justice Reads Historic Decision; Vote Was Unanimous

Ruling Does Not End Segregation At Once; Further Hearings Set To Decide How to Halt Practice

By HERB ALTSCHULL

WASHINGTON, May 17 (AP)—The Supreme Court ruled today that the states of the nation do not have the right to separate Negro and white pupils in different public schools.

By a unanimous 9-0 vote, the high court held that such segregation of the races is unconstitutional.

Chief Justice Warren read the historic decision to a packed but hushed gallery of spectators nearly two years after Negro residents of four states and the District of Columbia went before the court to challenge the principle of segregation.

The ruling does not end segregation at once. Further hearings were set for this fall to decide how and when to end the practice of segregation. Thus a lengthy delay is likely before the decision is carried out.

Dean Acheson, secretary of state under Former President Harry Truman, was in the courtroom to hear the ruling. He called it "great and statesmanlike."

Atty. Gen. Brownell was also present. He declined comment immediately. Brownell and the Eisenhower administration, like Truman's, opposed segregation.

For years 17 Southern and "border" states have imposed

presented: Does segregation of children in public schools solely on the basis of race, even though the physical facilities and other 'tangible' factors may be equal, deprive the children of the min-

9 The action or state of setting someone or something apart from other people or things or being set apart. For example, the enforced separation of different racial groups in a country, community, or establishment. During the early part of the 20th century, blacks were segregated from whites.

The concept of poverty also had an influence on my life. Being "poor," however, is a relative concept. My family was poor; we just didn't know it. By all conventional standards, we were poor, but when you're poor, you don't know what you don't know. It's the water you swim in.

A little story can help understand the mental model of the poor.

Two young fish were swimming along one day minding their own business when they noticed another older fish coming toward them. As the older fish passed by them, he nods at them and says, "How's the water?"

One of the other fish said to the other, "What's water?"

The point of the fish story is merely that the most obvious, important realities are often the ones hardest to see. We simply are not always conscious of the totally obvious.

So where does our most basic understanding of the world come from? Is it just somehow hardwired, like height or shoe size? How we construct meaning is a matter of culture—the water we swim in. From this foundation, my journey began.

fam·i·ly

ˈfam(ə)lē

a group consisting of parents and children living together in a household.

se·cu·ri·ty

si-ˈkyu̇r-ə-tē

the quality or state of being secure:

such as a: freedom from danger: a feeling of safety

b: freedom from fear or anxiety

CHAPTER 3

The Journey Begins

I Was Number Eight

I was last child of eight children born to Hattie Lucille Jackson Garmon (38) and Joe Franklin Garmon (45). My ancestry DNA test reported a German and Scandinavian lineage. I had been told all my life I had some Native American blood, but the DNA test put that rumor to rest. There was, however, a little novelty to my early life. Interestingly enough, I had a niece and nephew who were born before me. My oldest brother, Jimmy, and his wife, Faye, already had their first daughter, Robin, and just a month before me a son, Larry. My mother, my brother's wife, and my sister Patsy were all expecting at the same time. I grew up with nieces and nephews who were like brothers and sisters or best friends—Robin, Larry, Ricky, Anita, Lisa, and others.

Freddie with his parents, Joe and Hattie Garmon 1957

My sister Betty Jean was 9 years old when I was born and thus was at home and helped Mama take care of me much of my first years. I cried a great deal during the first days and weeks of my life. They later learned that my collar bone had been broken at birth!

Life was a struggle from the very beginning. I was a slow-cooking, 44-week baby, which played a part in a life-threatening delivery and the ensuing broken collar bone. The doctor was not sure I was going to live. In fact, the doctor forewarned my dad that it was likely neither my mom nor I would survive. But WE did!

The first nine years of my life revealed what I thought to be typical of other kids and families.

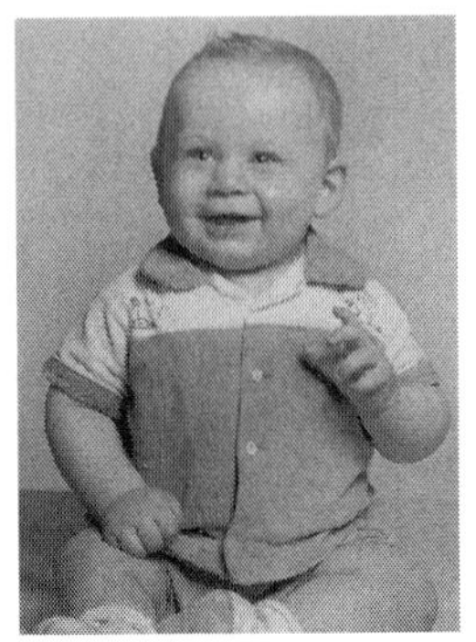
Freddie 1958

Freddie with his mom and dad
Easter 1963

My dad was a brick mason by trade and my brothers Jimmy and J. F. (John Franklin) worked with Daddy (as we called our father). Mama, as we affectionately referred to our mother, was a stay-at-home mom. A six-room block house, built by my dad, and its small yard, was my world.

Daddy learned his trade during the 1920s, just after the end of World War I, making it only to the third grade before quitting school at 9 years old. Daddy told me that he quit school to work and help the family.

Daddy worked extremely hard from sunup to between 5 and 6 p.m. every day, oftentimes leaving home before daylight to get ahead of the heat that came later in the day. I distinctly remember watching the local weather forecaster give each day's forecast on our black-and-white, three-channel television with "rabbit ears." The weather was critical to Daddy's ability to work.

Mama and I would stay home. I played outside much of each day, living in a land of childhood imagination. Summers were hot. We had screen doors at the front and back of the house to pull air throughout the muggy house. We placed electric fans in a few strategic windows to help circulate the air.

Winters were cold. We had an oil furnace in the center of the house to heat our entire home. We didn't get out much either. I remember Saturday being a big day in the week. It was the day we went to the grocery store to get the coming week's groceries. All the stores were locally owned, "mom and pop" businesses. I especially remember the toy display and the meat department at what was our neighborhood grocery store, "Norman's Market."

When time for school came, I attended Lakeview Elementary School

just a short walk from our home. Lakeview was a neighborhood school, and all the children that attended Lakeview came from within walking distance. I distinctly remember grades 1-3 with Mrs. Todd, Mrs. Berryhill, and Mrs. Chapman. Early every morning I'd meet other neighborhood kids and walk together to school. My, how things have changed! I can't imagine doing that with 6- to 8-year-olds today.

Fred's Family
Top: L to R - Virginia (Jenny), Patsy Ruth, J. F., JoAnn, Joe Franklin, Hattie Lucille
Bottom: Nancy, Betty Jean, Freddie Thomas (not pictured: Jimmy)

During those formative years, I kind of felt like the mascot of the family—not one of the grandchildren and not really one of the brothers and sisters either. I was like an only child living at home with Mama and Daddy. Betty Jean must have been around a great deal, but I don't remember her. I do remember Sundays being my favorite day because all the family would come to our house for Sunday dinner. Fried chicken and country vegetables were staples of this meal. Children always got to eat first, then the adults.

While I don't remember much about those first few years, I will never forget three major marker events, two of which effected the public psyche of our entire nation and the other which altered Daddy, Mama, and me at home.

The Beatles and Ed Sullivan

The first was a television show that my youngest sister, Betty Jean, wanted to watch—the North American debut of the Beatles on the Sunday evening *Ed Sullivan Show,* February 9, 1964. It was a major deal for her, but Mama was totally against watching it on our TV. Betty did see it, but she had to go next door to Uncle Doc and Aunt Cleone's house to watch it with our cousin David.

Daddy and I watched "Bonanza" with Ben, Hoss, Little Joe, Adam and Hop Sing at our house.

The Assassination of President Kennedy

The second event impacted not only the United States but the entire world. I was playing in the floor with my army men and medieval knights when the morning TV program Mama was watching was interrupted with "breaking news." It was the assassination of President John F. Kennedy on Friday, November 22, 1963, at 11:30 a.m. EST. Even at 6 years old I sensed the gravity of the event.

Chicago Tribune

ASSASSIN KILLS KENNEDY
LYNDON JOHNSON SWORN IN

GOVERNOR OF TEXAS WOUNDED; MARXIST ACCUSED OF MURDER

President John F. Kennedy in Dallas, Texas Parade
Friday, November 22, 1963

Daddy Disabled From Work

The third event was of a more personal nature and involved Daddy's health. The years of construction work, lifting brick and block, had taken its toll on Daddy's back. It all came to a head when Daddy underwent surgery for gallstones. In those days, this type of surgery involved cutting a person almost in half. Daddy was forced into retirement and never laid brick again.

The ripple effect required a financial adjustment. Daddy applied for Social Security benefits and we scaled down to live on three meager Social Security checks per month; Daddy's, Mama's, and mine. Mama and I received small checks as dependents of Daddy's years of work.

Daddy was a proud provider of our family. He quickly learned he could supplement our income and earn a certain amount of additional income each year, so he took control of a local gas station in partnership with his brother-in-law, Uncle William.

I remember going to the gas station with Mama to visit Daddy. Daddy would always give me an RC Cola and a snack—sometimes a Moon Pie, sometimes a huge dill pickle, sometimes a sausage. The pickles and sausages set on the inside counter in big glass jars. Gas stations back then were called "service stations." The nomenclature was due to the "service" each customer received during each and every experience—pumping your gas, checking your tire pressure, examining your water and motor oil levels. The attendant would also clean your front window—very different from today's self-service model.

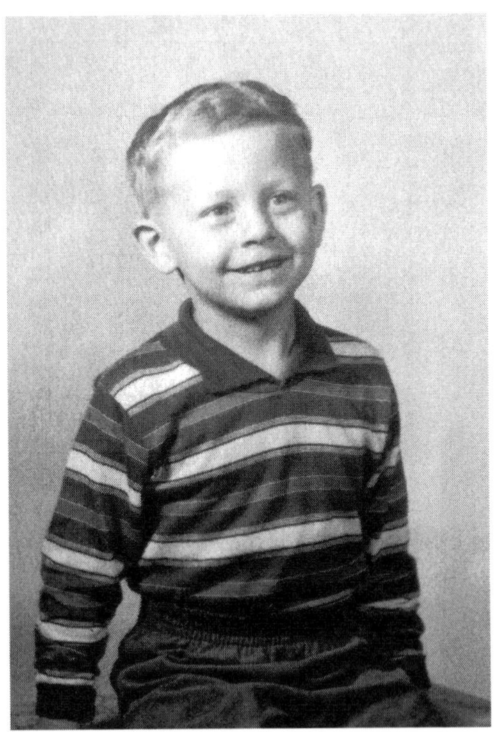

Freddie 1963
5 years old

grief

deep sorrow, especially that
caused by someone's death.

sorrow, misery, sadness, anguish, pain, distress,
heartache, heartbreak, agony, torment, affliction,
suffering, woe, desolation, dejection, despair

CHAPTER 4

Two Watershed Family Crises

Crisis #1

On Thursday, February 2, 1967, Lyndon Johnson was president, and most of the United States was listening to "I'm a Believer" by the Monkees.

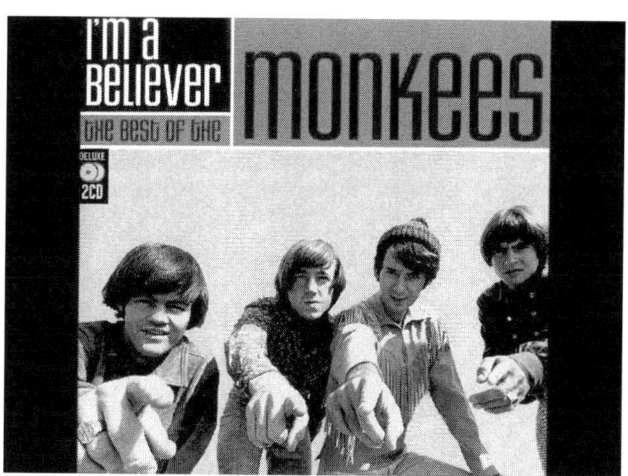

This particular Thursday seemed like every other Thursday that had preceded it. I was put to bed around 9 p.m. and was fast asleep. Sometime around 11 p.m. I was suddenly awakened by the sound of police and family members frantically moving throughout our home. The blue lights of police cars and red lights from an ambulance were reflecting off the walls. I could hear Mama hysterically crying and screaming, "Oh no, not my baby girl!" and Daddy responding angrily as the police questioned him.

My older cousin, David, who lived next door, was given charge of me and instructed to take me to his house for the rest of the night. As I was leaving the house, I heard that my sister, Betty Jean, 18 years old, had been shot and killed in our front yard.

Betty Jean had recently gotten married to a local young man and had evidently gotten into an argument while sitting in their car in our front yard. Somehow they had gotten my dad's pistol from the house and, during a struggle, Betty was shot in the chest. The bullet hit her in the heart, and death was almost immediate. No one really knows for sure what happened in that car that night, but the loss of our sister and my parent's youngest daughter rocked our world.

The next few days were a blur, filled with intense emotion, grief and community support. The tradition at that time among many families was to bring deceased family members home during visitation times instead of having them lie in state at a funeral home or church. So Betty Jean's coffin set for a full day and evening in our front living room as family and friends came in and out all throughout the day and night. I remember being very confused and lonely. I did not understand what was going on, and I seemed to get lost in the crowd and grief of the moment.

The next few months after Betty's funeral were filled with something worse than grief. Downright misery and depression permeated the atmosphere as Daddy and Mama attempted to make sense of life again. The grief and sorrow came in "waves" with intense feelings of numbness, shock, and disbelief. The reality hit hard; Betty Jean was gone.

Crisis #2

Four months went by. The last week of June 1967 was a hot summer morning. Mama and I were at home alone. I remember hearing her make a phone call. She stood in the front living room as she dialed the black hard-wired telephone. Her words scared me as she told the person on the other end of the conversation that she needed to be taken to the hospital immediately.

Mama was admitted to the hospital later that afternoon. She was in terrible pain, losing a great deal of blood. The diagnosis was quick and devastating; she had cancer, and it was out of control. Mama was given five weeks to live.

Several days later, my oldest brother, Jimmy, took me to the hospital to visit Mama. Due to the strict rules concerning minors and visiting hours, Jimmy took me up the stairs through an exit. The picture of my mother lying in that hospital bed surrounded by flowers is forever etched in my memory. It had only been nine or 10 days since I had last seen her, but she was now in terrible shape. The cancer had taken its toll. She called me "little boy blue" and asked me to come stand beside her. I remember being so afraid and so confused ... again. Mama held me by the hand and spoke to me about love and promise. She knew she was leaving this world, and her biggest concern in the world was me. I later learned that Mama was concerned about Daddy's ability to care for me. Time would reveal that her apprehension was justified.

Although the family had been told Mama could live five weeks, on Friday, July 7, 1967, two weeks from the time she was hospitalized, Mama died.

Just five months from Betty Jean's tragic death, my dad lost his wife and the rest of us lost our mother. How could this be possible? Our family had been so large, and everything seemed to be going well. Now everything seemed to be falling apart.

Most families have a member who serves as the "oak tree" of the family. The person who holds it all together. The person everyone looks to as the stabilizer and foundation of the household. That person in our family was

Mama, and now she was gone. Ironically, on that very day in 1967, the Beatles released "All You Need Is Love," and we found ourselves in great need of it. Our family was still grieving and dealing with the loss of Betty Jean, and now that wound was reopened with the death of Hattie Lucille—Daddy's wife, our mother. A tough situation had been made worse; insult was added to injury.

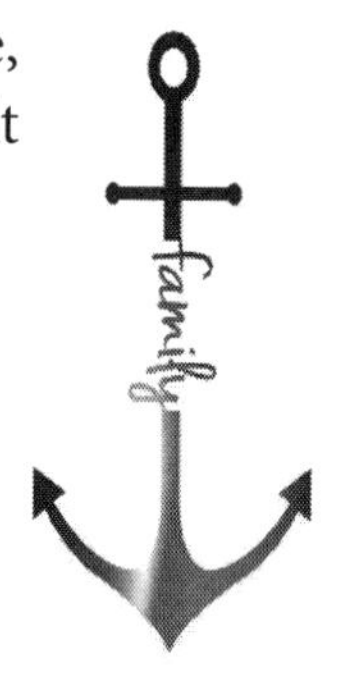

Someone said that "family is the anchor that holds us through life's storms." But what do you do when your family is the one being torn apart by the storms of life?

Mama too was brought home for viewing. She lay in state in our living room for one day before the funeral, and again family and friends found time to try and console our family. I remember going into the bathroom, standing on the tub, looking into the mirror above the bathroom sink, crying, and asking, *Why my mom? Why is my mom gone?*

The Pain of Grief Does Strange Things

I do not remember much of the next two years. My fourth and fifth grades at Lakeview Elementary School are fuzzy. For instance, I don't remember my fourth and fifth-grade teachers at all. During these two years, my dad and I lived alone at 2916 Clyde Drive in Charlotte. The few memories I do have during those two years still hurt deeply today:

- Coming home from school to a house full of drunks, men and women
- Eating sandwiches of fried bologna and cheese on white bread
- Drinking cold milk
- Asking for a dollar so I could go alone to the Wagon Wheel Grill to get a cheeseburger, fries, and Cheerwine (a cherry cola drink)
- Being bullied by a classmate on the way home from school almost every day
- Walking around the neighborhood on weekends asking if anyone had seen my dad
- Ringing the bell for the Salvation Army—standing outside a local store or the mall asking for money.

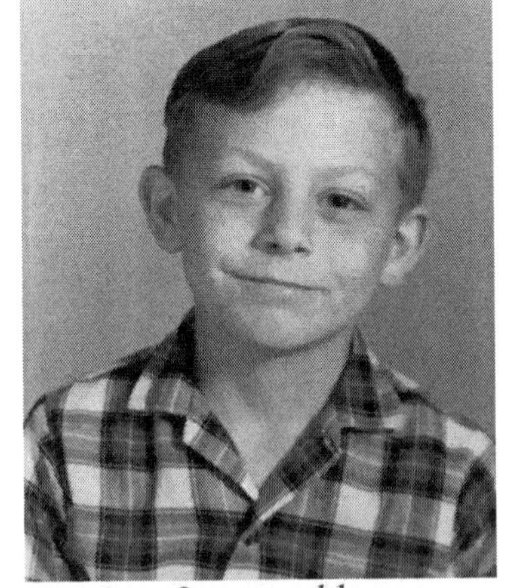
9 years old

I understand we have amazing psychological mechanisms that automatically protect us when life gets unbearable. And I guess that 9-year-old little boy just could not endure any more of the pain, insecurity, loneliness, and hopelessness that loss had brought.

During my adult years, and especially as I became aware of personal growth and leadership development principles, I learned about fundamental psychology. Educational experiences have become, and still are, part of my continual journey toward inner healing. For instance, the processes that keep unwanted thoughts from entering our consciousness are known as defense mechanisms and include suppression and repression mechanisms. Defense mechanisms are a part of our everyday life.

Suppression is the voluntary form of repression. It is the conscious process of pushing unwanted, anxiety-provoking thoughts, memories, emotions, and fantasies out of our awareness.

Repression, on the other hand, involves forgetting something bad, the unconscious process of excluding painful memories, thoughts, and impulses from consciousness.

In some cases, individuals experience a traumatic event that triggers such a potent stress response that it causes the memory or memories associated with that event to be repressed. The potency of the event exceeds their natural ability to cope with the emotions associated with the traumatic event. Such emotions are often overpowering, leading to intense sensations of anger, depression, fear, guilt, hopelessness, or shame—all negative emotions. In this case, there is a "gap" or lapse in memory surrounding the time of the trauma. The individual knows they endured the traumatic event, but they are so emotionally overwhelmed and physiologically "fried" that memory of the traumatic event is submerged beneath conscious perception. The problem is that as much as we consciously and unconsciously try to forget, there are still situations that bring the effects of the trauma rushing back at us.

For some individuals, triggers associated with the traumatic event(s) can cause these negative emotions to hit them like a ton of bricks, so hard that the experience interferes with their cognitive functions.

From repression, it is easy for a person to move into regression—one little "g" makes all the difference. In regression, particularly under conditions of stress, a person can revert back to a childlike emotional state in which unconscious fears, anxieties, and general "angst" reappear. It is a frightening experience to be an adult and be placed in a situation where you feel that traumatized little boy surface again.

"Do not throw your pearls to pigs. If you do, they may trample them under their feet, and turn and tear you to pieces"
(Matthew 7:6, *NIV*).

CHAPTER 5

Don't Cast Your Pearls Before Swine

Jesus told an interesting story in Matthew 7:6 (*NIV*)—"Do not throw your pearls to pigs. If you do, they may trample them under their feet, and turn and tear you to pieces."

I think I may have some insight into this wise statement. A pearl comes from an oyster. An oyster has a unique and marvelous ability to turn something that causes pain—an irritant, a grain of sand, into something precious—a pearl of great price. That oyster secretes a pearly luster over that which causes it pain. So it is that we too have this ability to take something that has caused us great pain and transform it into something bearable, even something good. Something that drives us forward, something that releases determination to change, to succeed.

Jesus' admonition here is to be careful with whom you share such experiences. His words of caution remind us, sadly, that an all too common human propensity is to hurt people with words. Humans have a tendency to say the most hurtful things to those they are the most close to, the people we love the most, that hurt them far deeper than we can possibly understand. Such deep pain has been described as "psychic agony."

You cannot control most of the major influences on your life, but you do have absolute control over how you choose to interpret them, what they mean to you. If you control the meaning of events in your life by creating as much value as you can, you will have a sense of purpose and personal power. On the other hand, if you deal with these events by devaluing yourself or others, you create a chronic sense of powerlessness, characterized by roller-coaster rides of emotion.

Rather than focus on the possible causes of pain and vulnerability, try to sort out what each hurtful incident means to you and what you can do to heal and improve. You can choose to crawl into a mental cave of self-pity or transform the pain into a driving force of good. The key is to funnel this energy toward a determination to improve.

We Do Not Experience Grief Alone

I wasn't alone in my struggle. My daddy too was overwhelmed by grief and was just trying to survive. Dad's way to deal with his grief was to retreat into a bottle of cheap wine. The days and months that followed Mom's death were filled with drunken stupors and unbearable nights as Daddy cried himself to sleep, calling out to and for *Mama*, as even my Daddy referred to her. *"Oh, Mama, oh, Mama, why did you leave me?"* I lay in the bed beside him, trying in my own 9- and 10-year-old way to let him know I was there and he was not alone. I would get as close to him as possible. I'm not sure he even knew I was there.

My Weekend Place of Sanctuary

I also have another memory of those days in 1967 and 1968: going to the Belvedere Theatre, sometimes on Friday night, but always, all day, every Saturday and Sunday.

The Belvedere Theatre on Rozzelle's Ferry Road in Charlotte was just a few blocks from our house. Twenty-five cents would get me in, five cents would get me popcorn, and another five cents would get me a Coke. This theatre, where my cousin David Freeman worked as projectionist, became my weekend sanctuary. I went to the movies every weekend. It was an escape from my lonely and insecure life. They played three movies twice a day on weekends, so I could literally stay all day and night, often spending time upstairs in the projection room with cousin David.

The Belvedere Theatre on Rozzles Ferry Road, Charlotte, NC

Remarkably, to this day I find great security and peace in just going to a movie and enjoying a bag of popcorn. I often go by a theatre and just purchase a bag of popcorn; it's like a bag of therapy.

Belvedere Theatre Today After Historical Renovations
(Makes my heart proud)

Help Moves In

Two years later, the summer of 1969 brought a little help to the dysfunctional struggle Daddy and I were enduring. Patsy Ruth, one of my sisters, moved in with us at 2916 Clyde Drive, bringing her two children, Sharon and Mark. Once again, Sharon and Mark were more like siblings instead of nieces and nephews. In fact, Sharon was just six months younger than me. Patsy's husband, Lee Roy Gardner (Lee), was a soldier serving in Vietnam, so she thought this could be a help to everyone.

Fascinatingly, something of Patsy's plan worked. My memories begin again here.

Patsy in 1979

Change, Change! Stability, Please!

September 1969 brought another major change to my already topsy-turvy life. The federal government's desegregation plan finally made it to our neighborhood schools, and with it came forced busing as all the schools in Charlotte Mecklenburg County were integrated.

Desegregation Plan Brought Change to Charlotte

My sixth-grade school year, my last year in elementary school before moving to junior high school, would not be spent attending the Lakeview Elementary School where I had been for the past five years.

I was assigned to Thomasboro Elementary School, which required that I take a city bus every morning and afternoon to and from school.

I remember much more of my sixth-grade school year, so evidently the psychic agony was beginning to subside. I also remember my teacher, Mr. Knox, my first male teacher. Mr. Knox was one of those dedicated teachers who truly cared about each of his students. I'll never forget one particular act of service he made toward me.

First Memory of a Life-Role Leader

We were having a sixth-grade basketball competition event. Being on the team required several days of after school practice and the ability to get your own team uniform (primarily a blue t-shirt with a number on it). I figured out how to catch the last 5 o'clock bus home from school but could not think of a way to get that t-shirt.

I missed the bus the next two days, so I had to walk the entire five miles home—an inconvenience for a sixth-grader, but I made it. I can't imagine one of my grandchildren navigating neighborhoods and wooded areas alone, but I don't remember anyone in my family thinking it was a very big deal.

I was distraught the night before the basketball event because I wasn't able to get that blue t-shirt. I had settled in my heart that I wasn't going to participate in the event. I remember crying myself to sleep that night.

The next morning, when I got to class, to my surprise, I found a small brown paper bag placed beside my desk.

I looked inside and I found a blue t-shirt, a pair of blue shorts, and a set of blue knee pads. I guess I'll never know for sure, but I believe my teacher, Mr. Knox bought them for me and placed the bag by my desk.

I had to be *the* proudest little boy on the basketball court that afternoon. And even though no one from my family knew about it or was there to cheer me on, and even though I only played a few minutes of that game, something special happened in me that day.

Lots of Stuff Built Up Inside

My sister Patsy tried hard to help me, but her intervention was short-lived due to all the pain inside my heart and my inability to adjust to all the change. I remember vividly the day another sister, JoAnn, came and got me. She told me to get my clothes; I was going to live with her and her husband, Gene.

New Neighborhood, New Friends; Growing Up

The sixth grade came to an end, and summer break put me in touch with new friends in a new neighborhood. The west side of Charlotte had several teenage gangs, and one of the most active gangs was situated right in the heart of where JoAnn lived and where I had just moved. Most of those associated with this gang were between 13 and 20 years old, and between 40 and 50 people were within my primary circle of close relationships. The summer break, therefore, firmly established me as a young but tuff[10] new member.

JoAnn, now 30 years old, had just given birth to her first child, a beautiful little girl she named Tonya. Tonya had been born on Thursday, April 24, 1969. Richard Nixon was president, and the Fifth Dimension's "Let the Sunshine In" was the top song. Tonya would become a major person in my life, growing up in my shadow.

The new 1970 school year brought with it a new birthday; I was now a teenager—13 years old. And I was living with JoAnn, Gene, and little Tonya. I attended Spaugh Junior High School and walked to and from school every day. My sister, JoAnn, had decided to choose her battles with me and thus was somewhat liberal when it came to certain

10 Tuff—Cool, in a rugged, wrong-side-of-the-tracks way.

vices. One of them was smoking cigarettes. She did not put up a fuss upon learning that I was smoking. Just the opposite—she allowed it! So I started openly smoking at home and elsewhere when I was in the seventh grade and 13 years old.

The eight-track tape was popular and Credence Clearwater Revival was my favorite band with "Down on the Corner."

During the fall of 1970, I got caught up in a riot one night after a junior high school band competition and concert. The Civil Rights Movement had brought with it riots all throughout the South, and Charlotte was one of the hotbeds with riots taking place in downtown streets. Spaugh Junior High, and this particular concert, a "battle of the bands," became a catalyst for one of the most destructive riots.

In hindsight, it was easy to see that someone didn't think through the planning of this event because one of the bands in the competition was white and the other black. This chemistry was an accident just waiting to happen. The gym, where the musical competition was being held, was packed out, a real fire hazard but quite exciting. Hundreds were left standing outside. The evening went well until the winner was announced. At that point tempers quickly went nuclear on both sides. It was as if both parties were looking for a reason to start trouble.

I could not get out of there fast enough. I was already street smart enough to see that this event was falling apart fast. But in my attempts to get clear of the property, I got caught in the middle of it. In fact, so many angry people were on the school grounds that the police could not control the crowd.

The next thing I knew I was tripped and found myself on the ground being kicked and hit with fists, sticks, pipes, and belts. I didn't believe I was going to make it out of there, when from out of nowhere, another student's dad grabbed me and pulled me and his two teenage daughters behind a nearby building.

I was bruised, cut, and bloody, but I was alive and able to walk home.

Junior High School Years

The seventh and eighth grades (1970-1971) were spent learning, but not learning from within the local school system. I was learning how to make it on the streets. Strangely, belonging to the street gang brought a tremendous sense of family and security and filled an empty void. What I lost when Betty Jean and Mama died and Daddy retreated into a bottle, I thought I had found again.

Along with this newfound substitute family came a culture of new and dysfunctional behaviors. Research tells us low income, a broken home, and a culture of violence all work together to help create conditions that deviate from social norms. Adolescents, in particular, join gangs because the gang acts both as a surrogate family and provides a sense of belonging, power, control, and prestige, all things commonly identified as absent in childhood. Basically, we took care of each other. For me, being part of this neighborhood group meant I would never again be alone in the world.

Innovative Ways to Get High

We became innovative at finding ways to get high. When we didn't have marijuana, we sniffed glue or gas.

Our favorite hangout was a pool hall on Tuckaseegee Road. There I learned to play a fairly good game of pool and even as a young teenager could make a good amount of money gambling. Part of the skill set involved learning how to size up your opponent.

One thing led to another, and money from pool winnings purchased more popular and more expensive drugs. Beer and liquor led to marijuana that led to mescaline and LSD (Beatles: Lucy in the Sky with Diamonds). The deeper I got into the gang culture, the more my behavior and looks changed. The descent into deeper dysfunction was initially visible in my school behavior and report cards. I let my hair grow to my shoulders, onto my back, and pierced my left ear. (This was a sign of rebellion in the 1960s and 70s.) One pair of blue jeans, a t-shirt, and tennis shoes were the only clothes I owned.

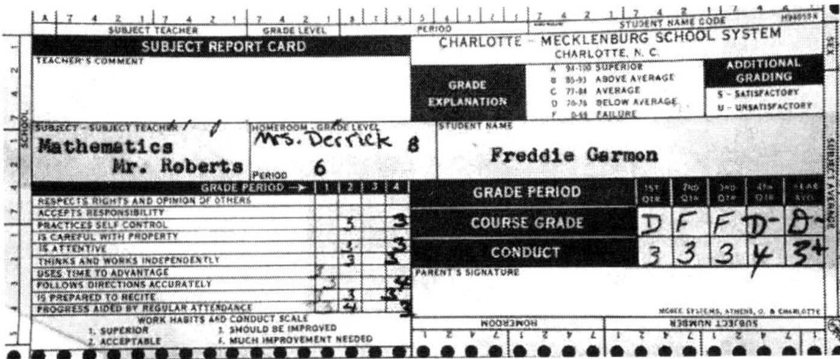

SUBJECT REPORT CARD

CHARLOTTE - MECKLENBURG SCHOOL SYSTEM
CHARLOTTE, N. C.

GRADE EXPLANATION: A 94-100 SUPERIOR; B 85-93 ABOVE AVERAGE; C 77-84 AVERAGE; D 70-76 BELOW AVERAGE; F 0-69 FAILURE

ADDITIONAL GRADING: S - SATISFACTORY; U - UNSATISFACTORY

TEACHER'S COMMENT

SUBJECT - SUBJECT TEACHER: Mathematics, Mr. Roberts

HOMEROOM - GRADE LEVEL: Mrs. Derrick 8

PERIOD: 6

STUDENT NAME: Freddie Garmon

GRADE PERIOD →	1	2	3	4
RESPECTS RIGHTS AND OPINION OF OTHERS				
ACCEPTS RESPONSIBILITY				
PRACTICES SELF CONTROL		3		3
IS CAREFUL WITH PROPERTY				
IS ATTENTIVE		3		3
THINKS AND WORKS INDEPENDENTLY		3		3
USES TIME TO ADVANTAGE				
FOLLOWS DIRECTIONS ACCURATELY				3
IS PREPARED TO RECITE		3		3
PROGRESS AIDED BY REGULAR ATTENDANCE		4		3

WORK HABITS AND CONDUCT SCALE: 1. SUPERIOR; 2. ACCEPTABLE; 3. SHOULD BE IMPROVED; 4. MUCH IMPROVEMENT NEEDED

GRADE PERIOD	1ST QTR	2ND QTR	3RD QTR	4TH QTR	YEAR AVG
COURSE GRADE	D	F	F	D-	D-
CONDUCT	3	3	3	4	3+

PARENT'S SIGNATURE

The combination of doing drugs, dealing drugs, and gambling by shooting pool kept money in my pocket and friends happy. I felt like somebody. A dysfunctional somebody, but a somebody. In fact, I didn't know there was any other way of life. I was simply attempting to find out how to be successful in the only culture and life I knew. It is now evident that I did not possess the maturity or critical thinking skills required to fully understand the danger and negative consequences of my involvement. But when it's the "water you swim in" you simply do not know any better.

Even at this early age (13-14), my love for people and naturally likeable personality allowed me to become friends and navigate relationships with people twice and three times my age. These relationships developed contacts and connections that enabled me to purchase small quantities of drugs that I started to sell (called "dealing on the street").

Solipsism
is the view that
I am the only person or mind which exists.

CHAPTER 6

My Psychedelic Revolution

The 1960s and 1970s have been proudly defined as a "Psychedelic Revolution" and an unfortunate pop fad. The memories associated with my experiences during the early 1970s still frighten me. Someone once asked me, "What were you thinking?" My answer? "I wasn't. I was busy surviving."

The idea of a young teenager thumbing rides (hitchhiking) up and down Interstate 85 from Charlotte to Atlanta is simply terrifying. Waking up in abandoned apartment buildings with dozens of others after a drug-induced night happened many times. Being caught outside in the cold in early dark mornings (3-6 a.m.) caused me on several occasions to seek shelter in the woods and even in a ditch. The possibility of freezing to death crossed my mind on several occasions.

I also experienced on several instances what is referred to as the dreaded "bad trip" brought on by taking hallucinogenic drugs like LSD, mescaline, or "magic mushrooms" ('shrooms). These mind-altering occurrences caused me to endure more than one terror-filled evening. These episodes were part of a larger countercultural context that were purported to be "tools of enlightenment." They were, in reality, cheap and dangerous ways to stay "messed up" and numb, yet appear to be cool. But these drug-induced "freak outs" often messed with my mind and scared me to death.

A "Bad Trip": Solipsism and the Mind's Creation

On a summer day in 1970, a large number of our gang (30-40 people) gathered at a local public park. During the early afternoon we started sniffing gas, which at that time was a popular form of inhalant abuse. Intoxication effects from sniffing or inhaling gasoline is very similar to that of consuming alcohol, but with the additional effect of hallucinations. Within minutes of sniffing gasoline, the person becomes intoxicated and within just one minute the person can experience a wide array of effects: euphoria, numbness, disorientation, hallucinations, dizziness, and disassociation from the environment.

Caution: Read at Your Own Risk

The gas can was passed to me. A group of us were sitting on the ground in the middle of a grassy field. I placed my hands firmly around the opening in the can and inhaled deeply five or six times. Even before I put the can on the ground, I started "getting a buzz." I could sense the effects of the gas.

I leaned back onto one arm and extended my legs out in front of me. Suddenly everything around me disappeared, and I found myself floating in a world of dark nothingness as my entire visual field became a vivid hallucination I couldn't control.

All I could see was from my chest down to my feet and my feet seemed to be 100 yards away, long and skinny, disappearing into the horizon. I could still hear the loud noises (laughing and talking) from my group of friends who were surrounding me, many of whom were also high from sniffing the gas.

To say the very least, I was panicked and terrified. The hallucinations had started with simple "trails" and other minor visuals.

A "trail," in reference to drug induced hallucination, is a visual illusion where a person sees a persistent recurrence of a visual image after the image has been removed. It is like waving your hand in front of your face and seeing 20 or more hands follow in succession after your hand has stopped moving.

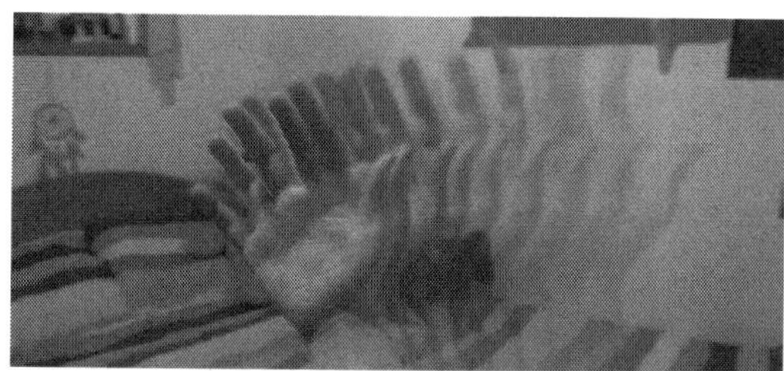

I was paralyzed. I couldn't move any part of my body except my head and neck. As I turned my head, swiveling left then right, bodiless faces began appearing in the distance all around me. They started appearing in the far upper right of my peripheral vision as I turned my head. Then more appeared on my left side. As they appeared I could hear them laughing in an evil sort of way. Their laughs were echoing and fading away. At one point, scores of faces of different sizes and distances from me appeared in the space all around me.

People often talk about the interesting, hyper-alert, and even fascinating, euphoric experiences associated with drug use. But you seldom hear about the hellish experiences that are just as possible. I did not have the maturity or the inner psychological resources to center myself so the experience just kept spiraling out of control. Every moment seemed to last a lifetime, and I was certain I was dying. This was it.

Insult was added to injury when the faces, in unison, started repeating the phrase, "You're going to die, you're going to die, die, die, die!" Simultaneously, I could feel a huge crushing weight on my feet way out in the distance. It felt as if a monumental ball of lead was rolling over my feet and ankles and moving slowing but with resolve over my legs toward my waist, chest, and ultimately to my head. I was certain that I would die if that ball made it to my head. Just as the ball, and the unbelievable terror coming with it, got to my neck, the voices stopped their chanting, an eerie silence developed, and one face directly in front of me said, "We're going to give you one more chance."

In that moment, I was thrust back into reality. Two friends were lying on me and I pushed them off as if they were feathers. I jumped to my feet, visibly shaken, attracting the attention of everyone around me. They recognized that something deeply disturbing had just happened to me.

I had experienced a complete altered reality. What seemed like an hour or more, was actually no more than a few minutes. It would take years to unpack that experience. I walked away from that "trip" with the overarching belief and message that I was truly and universally *alone*. Nothing could have been more devastating to me. There could not have been a more damaging message given to one who already suffered from major loss, deep grief, and the insecurities that were outcomes of those experiences.

I later learned that Solipsism is the name given to one of the most dangerous ideologies that exists and could be one of the biggest lies ever told. This mind virus is so prevalent and insidious that it has infected the consciousness of many people in various ways. For some, it keeps them from seeking truth—the one thing that could set them free. For others, it drives them further toward a dysfunctional and egotistical emersion into narcissism and self-absorption. And for others, like me, it drives you deeper into a realm of loneliness and insecurity that can prompt horrifying nightmares.

This "trip" was similar to nightmares or night terrors I had while growing up. I would dream of being wrapped and bound with hundreds of feet of different colored wires and imprisoned in a deep hole with no way out. Sometimes I would remember the dreams the next morning; sometimes I would not. Sometimes I would also be semiconscious while the night terror was happening. I grew out of those dreams, but the "trip" vividly awakened once again the foundations of those fears.

The mind is a mysterious thing. The things it can do are both fascinating and disturbing. Years later, at 44 years old, I was studying PhD literature on leadership and came across this fascinating term and concept that immediately took me back to this solitary summer day and that traumatic experience.

Solipsism

The belief that you are the only person that exists and you only exist in your mind. There it was. A word, a concept representing an idea that I had wrestled with every day for the past 30 years. I continued reading.

You are not alone. Average people like you and me experienced solipsism as a child (infant solipsism). And solipsism is so common and convincing that there is even a solipsism syndrome.

It is amazing how certain disclosures of TRUTH—an epiphany, illuminating discovery, realization or disclosure—can so profoundly bring a release of stress and anxiety.

Bizarre Places and Cold Ditches

My independent and out-of-control life took me to a lot of bizarre places and frightening situations. My group of friends and I were constantly looking for cheap places to hang out, crash, and have a good time. Most of these places were low-cost rental apartments or houses with virtually no furniture and just a few mattresses on the floor. Doing drugs doesn't lend itself to caring about much more than the moment. Furniture, food, and other things are just "stuff" that doesn't really matter. One item, however, that was very important was music; thus, the stereo. A sound machine with large, loud speakers. We were never without a sound machine. After all, what good was a drug-induced trip without the appropriate background music, *e.g.*, Black Sabbath, Led Zeppelin, ZZ Top, Alice Cooper?

I remember being stoned one night and tripping on some hallucinogenic drug (probably acid). It must have been 5 or 6 a.m. when I felt someone grab me by the ankle and begin to literally drag me across the floor and through the apartment. My older sister, Nancy, had been worried about me and finally got a friend to tell her where I was. Funny thing was, the apartment was wall-to-wall with others tripping too, but no one seemed to even notice or care about what was happening to me. Nancy stood me up on the front porch of the apartment and walked me to her car. She took me home, but it wasn't long before I was gone again.

On another occasion, a friend and I thumbed a ride several hours away into the North Carolina mountains to a rodeo where we heard there was plenty of free drugs. We had no way to verify this rumor; we knew no one there and we didn't much care. It was just another insane adventure in a topsy-turvy life. Nothing about my life at that time made any sense, nor did it contain any rhyme or reason. I was just existing from day to day.

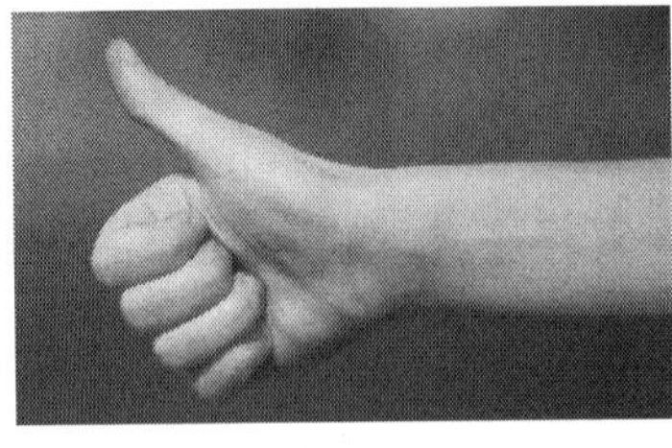

We leap-frogged from car to car and finally made it to the rodeo. Sure enough, we found the rodeo, some friends and some free drugs. We got stoned out of our minds and lost track of time, which, looking back, must have been one of the desired outcomes. Daytime gave way to night, and night led into the wee hours of the morning. Sometime after midnight I began to realize just how cold it gets in the mountains during the predawn hours. Even though it was mid-July, it felt like it was freezing, and all I was wearing was a pair of jeans and a t-shirt. We had nowhere to spend the night, so the only alternative was to try to hitchhike back home. It must have been around 3 a.m. when I decided to seek shelter in a nearby ditch just off the side of the highway. I thought I was going to freeze to death. I laid curled up in that ditch till the sun came up; then we started thumbing rides again.

There is no losing in jiu jitsu.
You either win or you learn.
We all need a little more
Jiu jitsu in our lives.

CHAPTER 7

Learning to Fight

Being a member of a street gang had its social benefits, but it also had its liabilities. I learned quickly that both were par for the course—normal and expected, given the circumstances. Life in a social network like this requires toughness. It's Darwin's Survival of the Fittest applied to relationships on the street. There was most definitely a social hierarchy, and members were constantly fighting to preserve their place in it, both literally and figuratively.

Life within the lower-class culture I was brought up in required competition and struggle just to survive. I, however, am by nature very competitive but not combatant. Competition, in my mind, did not involve fists, hurting someone else, or getting hurt. Nonetheless, several times, seemingly from out of nowhere, I found myself having to fight and sometimes fight a friend. The reasons were usually ambiguous and confusing, often simply the whim and crazy impulse of another alpha male who wanted to cause a little trouble or create personal entertainment. At other times, someone's fragile ego or determination to gain status within the group was the impetus.

I don't remember ever losing a fight, but then that depends on how you define "lose." I vividly remember walking away from fights hurt, in pain, bleeding, not wanting to do it again. But I assure you, my opponent regretted having started the scuffle as well. Most fights I got in didn't last long. The main reason involved a lesson I learned early on. My strategy going into a fight was simple: win. My tactic[11] or actual means I used to gain that objective was called a "sucker punch." A sucker punch is a blow given to another person without warning; it comes from out of nowhere—

11 The terms *tactic* and *strategy* are often confused: *tactics* are the actual means used to gain an objective while *strategy* is the overall campaign plan.

the recipient is not ready for it. By using this tactic, you usually win the fight before it ever begins, stunning and disorienting your opponent, allowing you to do enough damage so as to finish the fight swiftly.

A Single-Fight Contest

The Friday night was cold, and our gang was gathered at a newly opened teen hangout called "The Last Resort" around 10 p.m. The Last Resort was a ministry created by a local Baptist Church located on Tuckaseegee Road in Charlotte. The church had taken a house located on the property next to the church and renovated it for use as a teenage weekend gathering destination. They had done a great job, and their desire to give local teens a place to hang out on weekends was working extremely well, perhaps too well. On this particular Friday night, more than 100 teens were on the property, most of whom could never get inside the small house and most of whom were members of our gang. The church workers frankly were unprepared and overwhelmed.

Suddenly several cars and a van pulled into the parking lot across the street from the teen house. Fifteen or 20 members of a rival gang got out of the vehicles and proceeded to challenge our gang to a single fight contest. A great deal of verbal banter and teasing had taken place between the two groups for weeks leading up to this night. They wanted to settle the quarrel without having an all-out gang fight. The two leaders seemed to agree with this method and immediately turned to choose who would fight. The other gang leader turned and quickly asked one of his group to step forward. He then said to him, "Choose who you want to take on." The guy looked straight at me and said, "Him." I was stunned. What in the world? Why me? But there was no time for thinking. This was happening, and I had no choice.

A huge circle gathered in that parking lot, and I found myself standing in the middle of it. I removed my jacket and stepped forward. The other guy turned away from me to remove his coat as well. When he turned back toward me, I met him with a sucker punch blow to his left jaw. He never knew what hit him. He went to the ground and was so stunned that he had to be assisted to walk away. The fight was over that fast, and the debate about which gang was top of the neighborhood hierarchy was settled. I was, for a night, the conqueror and hero.

Bob McCall, in his book *Lessons of Experience*, describes four primary methods for learning[12]: Experience, mentors, mistakes, and formal education. I learned the sucker-punch tactic along with every other ways of defending myself through experience. One primary experience cemented the tactic in my personal survival toolbelt.

I played pool (gambling via billiards) at two primary locations: a pool hall on Tuckaseegee Road and the Freedom Drive bowling alley where there were several pool tables in a separate room. On this occasion I was shooting pool at the bowling alley. I was having a very good day and had won about $50 chiefly from one individual I had never seen before.

I was taking a break, sitting on a bar stool, smoking a cigarette, and watching a friend play a game of pool with another individual. A guy walked up to me and said someone wanted to talk with me outside. I naively followed the guy out the front doors where I noticed an old Mustang. A guy was in the driver's seat, and I recognized the guy in the back seat as the guy I had won the money from. The passenger door was open, and I bent down to look into the rear window of the car. I was suddenly hit in the side of the head by the guy standing beside me. I staggered backward several steps as the guy who hit me attempted to get inside the car. I was able to gather my senses much quicker than they had hoped and I immediately grabbed the open door and violently slammed it on the leg of the guy who had just hit me. He screamed in pain. I then put my full arm and fist inside the car and began swinging it back and forth from the front seat to the back seat; hitting one guy in the back of the head and the other guy in the face several times. The driver sped away with the passenger door swinging open. My right eye promptly swelled shut.

I came to a major conclusion that day, I learned a big lesson, and I paid a great price. The conclusion? "If you hit me, you'd better knock me out." The lesson? "Always be aware of those around you and their possible intentions." The price? I couldn't see out of my eye for days, and my friends thought it was very funny. But I was never sucker punched again. I used that tactic effectively on several occasions in the future.

Life on the street was always exposed and susceptible to unexpected occurrences. You have to learn quickly, and frankly, you have to have a

12 Kouses and Posner, in their book *The Leadership Challenge*, also describe the same four ways of learning.

certain amount of luck if you are to survive. A few examples serve to make this point.

Joey

Joey was a good friend. We fought on at least two occasions—once due to his own low self-esteem and another due to the whim of our gang leader. I won both squabbles, but we remained friends. Joey, however, enjoyed his drugs. He was always pushing the limits and attempting to get higher and higher. Joey was found dead in the front seat of another friend's car. He had taken what is called a "goofball," an upper and a downer drug at the same time, and was drinking alcohol on top of that. Joey choked to death on his own vomit. Joey had joked on several occasions about how he enjoyed walking close to the edge. That day he walked too close, and it was no joking matter.

Rocky

Rocky was another good friend. Rocky was killed early one morning while driving drunk and attempting to take a sharp curve too fast in his hot rod Ford. He wrapped his car around a big oak tree and died on impact.

Steve

Steve was several years older than me and was someone I looked up to. He was a person who on at least one occasion had my back in a tight and potentially harmful situation. Steve often frequented a local bar where his mother served as a waiter. On this particular evening, Steve witnessed a man touch his mother in an inappropriate manner. He told the man to keep his hands away from her. The man with no warning pulled a pistol and shot Steve at point blank range, killing him instantly.

Without a doubt, my story could have ended just like theirs. I often think about how fortunate I am to have lived through that season of my life.

My older brother J.F., knew the path I was on and understood it well. At times, he also attempted to intervene and try to stop me from destroying my life. I lived a life much like that of a vampire. We'd stay up all night and crash as the sun started coming up. We would subsequently sleep virtually all day. I recall one particular midday waking up to J.F. holding my left arm and screaming at me, "You've been up to it again, haven't you, boy?" He was looking at the tracks[13] in my arm. J.F. literally threw me over his shoulder, carried me out of our mobile home, and put me in the back seat of his car. He walked back to the porch and talked with Daddy for a few minutes, evidently telling Daddy about the rehabilitation home where he was going to admit me. But he never got me out of the driveway. I jumped out of the car and ran away. I was gone for several days this time before returning home. It must have been a frustrating and concerning time for Daddy and all my brothers and sisters. I was destroying my life, and there was nothing they could do to help me.

Fred and his brother, J.F.

13 *Track marks* are the tell-tale signs of chronic intravenous drug use. The act of drug injection is often referred to as "jacking up," "shooting up," or "slamming" and is typically identified with the use of heroin, cocaine, methamphetamines, and opiates.

I am the person your parents warned you about.

A phrase I painted on my ceiling.

CHAPTER 8

From the City to the Country

The eighth grade (1971) was another year of moving for me and my dad. Daddy had started getting a handle on his life by putting alcohol aside. He never really stopped grieving the loss of my mom, but he did learn to live with it.

My sister Patsy and her husband, Lee Roy, bought a home on Rush Avenue (still on the west side of Charlotte) and moved out of Daddy's house. A short time later Daddy sold the home place and moved in with Patsy.

At the same time my sister JoAnn began having trouble in her marriage. So she sent me to live with Patsy and Daddy on Rush Avenue. This move was only a few streets away so it did not disrupt my school experience, what little I was having. I continued to walk to Spaugh Junior High School every day and remained involved with the same friends and trafficked the same usual hangouts.

Sometime during the end of my eighth-grade year (1972), Daddy and I left Patsy's home and moved in with another sister, Nancy. Nancy and her husband, Jim, and their children, Debbie, Eddie, Alicia, and Ricky, lived on Rozzelle's Ferry Road in Charlotte, which was still on the west side of Charlotte.

Later that same year, JoAnn got divorced. So Daddy, JoAnn, and I came up with a plan to move away from Charlotte and start a new life. JoAnn's daughter, Tonya, was now 3 years old and would, of course, make the move with us. I was still getting my small Social Security check from Daddy's disability and that income became part of the financial plan. So we moved 30 miles north to Cabarrus County, North Carolina.

JoAnn and Daddy purchased a three-bedroom, single-wide trailer and a half-acre of land in what at that time seemed like the middle of nowhere. I know it may sound silly, but I was so proud of that mobile home. Patsy and JoAnn had enjoyed nice homes, but this trailer, for the first time in a long time, was *my* home, and I was so happy to make this move.

The official address of our new dirt road, country home, was Davidson, NC, but the geographical location was smack in the middle of several townships—Kannapolis, Davidson, Concord, and Mooresville, North Carolina. Our property was located just off Earnhardt's Lake Road, named after the NASCAR and stock car driving legion, Dale Earnhardt.

We moved our trailer onto our new property, down a dirt road, with aspirations and concerns about this new place. I distinctly remember the first time I used our telephone. I could hear someone else on the line, and it wasn't the person I had attempted to call. That's how I learned about a "party line." A telephone line shared by two or more parties on the same street. Telephone party-line service was common in sparsely populated areas and remote properties. This also helps describe more about where we had moved. Party lines provided no privacy in communication. They were also frequently used as a source of entertainment and gossip.

My sister JoAnn had started her own custom drapery business and had a small shop situated off Rozzelle's Ferry Road on North Hoskins Road, again located in west Charlotte (Drapery's by JoAnn). Amazingly, JoAnn juggled being a single mother with owning and operating her own business. She would drive her blue Ford Pinto the 30 miles to and from our new home every weekday morning and afternoon for 10 years.

Thirty miles doesn't sound like a long way to drive today. But in 1972 it seemed to us that we were moving to the other side of the world. Tonya, JoAnn's daughter, told me she remembered that Robin, my oldest brother's daughter, and my mama's sister, Vivian, helped take care of her in those early years. And Tonya said she remembered having a napping mat set on top of one of her mom's drapery cutting tables. I guess we all do whatever we have to do to make a living and care for our children—or at least we should.

A New Home, High School Beginning

In September 1971, I started the ninth grade at Northwest Cabarrus High School. The Charlotte School System included grades 7, 8, and 9 as junior high school and grades 10, 11, and 12 as high school. The Cabarrus County School system was different in that they started high school with the ninth grade. Consequently, with this move I was thrust a year earlier than expected into a high school environment. Moves like this bring with them tremendous potential for change—change for good or change that reinforces a dysfunctional path and its associated behavior(s).

My memories and feelings associated with this move were mixed. I liked the thought of having a place that Daddy, JoAnn, and I could again call our home, but I was hesitant and uneasy about leaving my family of friends in Charlotte.

I did, however, have a few unconscious yet visible signs and/or behaviors that instantly gave away the type of person I was and the group I would likely fit into at my new school. Long hair and earrings on young men in the 1960s and 70s was unconventional and part of a rebellious subculture. Personal branding is essential for the ongoing process of establishing a prescribed image or impression in the mind of others. My brand or "looks" was evidently extremely visible and clear within the context of the 1970s.

My first new friendships at school were established on the "smoking grounds" as they were called. The school had a morning and afternoon break, along with lunch, when we were allowed to smoke. It was a designated covered area at the back of the school.

My appearance opened the door to the type of friends I was accustomed to as my social group. Then my speech removed the door from its hinges.

Having access to drugs was immensely important to teenagers who were part of the drug culture. And I was from the "big city" of Charlotte with a network that included multiple opportunities to access almost any drug imaginable.

In these years I attended almost every rock-and-roll concert available. And the '70s provided plenty of venues to indulge this passion, especially when it came to weekend music festivals.

The following list represents most of the bands I saw during the 1970s, most of which were seen at huge weekend festivals:

> Led Zeppelin, Black Sabbath, Pink Floyd, AC/DC, The Who, Deep Purple, Aerosmith, Lynyrd Skynyrd, Fleetwood Mac, Queen, Allman Brothers, ZZ Top, Eagles, Credence Clearwater Revival, Blue Oyster Cult, Jethro Tull, Journey, Crosby, Stills, & Nash, Doobie Brothers, Van Halen, Grateful Dead,

> Beach Boys, Emerson, Lake and Palmer, Electric Light Orchestra, Foreigner, Sly and the Family Stone, Grand Funk Railroad, Steely Dan, Styx, Mot the Hoople, Frank Zappa, Santana, Uriah Heep, Alice Cooper, Chicago, Rod Stewart, Steve Miller Band, Three Dog Night, James Taylor, Bad Company, Moody Blues, Heart, Jefferson Starship, Nazareth, Badfinger, Marshall Tucker Band, Meat Loaf, Rare Earth, Brownsville Station, Charlie Daniels Band, Billy Preston.

My popularity exploded during my ninth-grade year. I was only 15 years old, but my ability to connect people in the new Cabarrus County area to drug resources in Charlotte opened many doors in numerous and unusual places, but this time with people much older and with many more financial resources. I became a middleman to many.

During this time, I painted a mural on the ceiling of my small bedroom in our single-wide mobile home. The mural was a painting depicting a hippy sitting on a large marijuana cigarette being held by a large hand. The hand was fully tattooed with an American flag. The larger-than-life hand was coming out of a city scape. Coming from this figure's mouth was this statement: "I am the person your parents warned you about."

Looking back now on the mural and that statement causes even me to question, "Why did I paint such a statement on my ceiling?" It had to capture my paradigm and mindset during that season of my life.

I received my ninth-grade, end-of-the-year report card in May 1972 with no surprise but a discouraging report. Out of six classes, I earned one "F" and five "zeros" primarily due to the number of days I had missed during that school year: I missed more days than I had attended. My dad had tried every morning to get me up and out the door, but most of the time I didn't make it. I was now destined to repeat the ninth grade. My life was a mess, and there seemed to be no turning around.

Fast forward through the summer to September 1972. It was supposed to be the beginning of my tenth-grade year, but instead I was scheduled to repeat the ninth grade having failed big time the previous year.

During football season, I sold weed to schoolmates after school and at the games. I was reckless. By mid-October, I knew the police were watching me and my close friends because on several occasions we were followed, even pulled over, and searched. I vividly remember one highway patrol officer spending a considerable amount of time talking to me and trying to convince me to walk away from my crazy and dangerous behavior. This would not be my last encounter with this man.

I remember the day well. I was in art class at school. Two police officers entered the room with Principal Robert (Bob) Garmon and asked for me. Once I was identified, they asked me to "come with them." I knew immediately this could not possibly be good news.

The officers escorted me to the school office where they explained that I was being arrested for selling drugs to students at the school. They put me in the police car, took me to the Concord Police Department and called my dad to come get me. JoAnn and Daddy arrived within an hour. The officers explained the gravity of the situation and that I would have to report to court on a given date. The officers also explained the possibilities of punishment and the caveat of my being a minor. They furthermore made it very clear that I was expelled from school and told not to set foot back on the school grounds. They released me into the custody of my dad and sister.

The next few weeks in October 1972 were pretty lonely since most of my friends were paranoid about coming around me, believing the police to still be watching me.

When life comes down around you
in smoldering ashes,
look around.
You just might
see grace.

CHAPTER 9

The First Sign of Grace

Daddy received a call requesting him to bring me to the Concord North Carolina Courthouse for a meeting. We made our way to the courthouse at the appointed time and found the two same police officers that arrested me along with an attorney. The attorney explained the situation and the options for going forward.

Nothing sounded very good to me. The attorney then explained they had done a little investigative research and found out that I had a sister living out of state in Missouri. My dad confirmed their statement, explaining that Patsy Ruth now lived in Fort Leonard Wood, Missouri, on the military base with her husband, Lee Roy Gardner, and her two children, Sharon and Mark.

The attorney and two police officers then told me that I had been officially expelled from school for the remainder of the year and proceeded to *tell me* I had one week to get out of North Carolina and spend at least this school year living with my sister, if she agreed, in Missouri.

Patsy and Lee Roy agreed to allow me to come. Within that same week Daddy took me to the Charlotte Douglas Airport where I would board an Eastern Airline's flight to Missouri.

I flew from Charlotte to St. Louis, arriving that evening. I then took a Greyhound bus down to Fort Leonard Wood. Patsy and her family met me at the bus station. Another chapter of my journey was underway.

I spent the remainder of that evening settling in to a bedroom I would be sharing with my younger nephew Mark.

Patsy wasted no time. Early the next morning she took me to the on-base junior high school to enroll me in the ninth grade. I remember

sitting in the school office waiting on the counselor and principal to meet with us. They called us in, and Patsy explained my situation to them.

Then another unexpected surprise!

What happened next I *never* expected. The counselor told Patsy they did not agree that I should be held back and that they were approving me for enrollment in the 10th grade at the off-base Waynesville High School. They gave us some official signed documents and off we went. We simply could not believe what had just happened. Wow!

I enrolled in Waynesville High School and immediately found several friends, a few who lived on base and had military parents and a few who lived off base in town. The problem was, once again, these friends enjoyed smoking weed. But the "good" news was they neither drank alcohol nor fooled around with hard drugs. Looking back, I think their choices had a great deal to do with their family structure and military culture. They were different, but I liked it.

I quickly found a place in the academic culture of the school as well. Something clicked. I enjoyed school and got engrossed in my art class. I knew I had a little skill at drawing, but this particular art teacher noticed and inspired me to develop my skill.

At the end of my year in Fort Leonard Wood at Waynesville High School, I had earned six A's on my report card. A complete turnaround in terms of my academic mindset and outcomes! At the same time, I had taken advantage of several *free* services offered to dependents living on the military base. I learned to play handball and earned belts and awards in judo and karate. These activities kept me busy and tapped into areas that motivated me in ways I'd never imagined.

I advanced rapidly in martial arts classes and earned a spot in the Missouri State Judo Tournament (Jiu-jitsu) that was held in St. Louis. I came away from that tournament earning second place in my age and weight division.

I remember a few months later when my brother, J. F., wanted to pick a little fight; he found himself on the ground. Martial arts remained a big part of my life for several years.

Five students from Waynesville High School were also chosen to represent our region at the Missouri State High School Art Festival, and I was one of the two boys and three girls. The festival was held at the Central Missouri State College, and I represented our region with pen-and-ink and pencil drawings. Both entries had to be drawn while on campus within a certain time limit.

I came away from the Missouri State Art competition with first place in the pen-and-ink category and second place in the pencil category.

My one-year mandatory trip to Missouri came to an end, and I was eager to go home to North Carolina. Much about me had not changed, but I had a unique experience that exposed me to a side of life I had never seen before. I had tapped into a part of me I didn't know existed.

What I did learn was that much of life is determined by those with whom you choose to hang around—your friends. I read somewhere that "Who you surround yourself with matters." Time would tell if I had internalized this lesson.

Going to Carolina

The next season of my life, particularly the five months from September 1973 to January 1974, contained a series of events that so impacted me as to literally change the trajectory of my life for decades to come. These five months redirected my steps to intersect with a future eventuality I did not know was even possible.

September 1973 took me back to North Carolina and Northwest Cabarrus High School. The year 1973 was an interesting point in history as well. Three important events dominated the news that year. First, Roe

V. Wade made abortion a U.S. Constitutional right. Second, the Watergate hearings in the U.S. Senate investigated whether activities in President Richard Nixon's re-election campaign were illegal and unethical. Third, the price of gasoline was 40 cents per gallon. In October 1973 the price of gasoline increased by 200 percent. The top three songs according to the Billboard Hot 100 were (1) "Tie a Yellow Ribbon Round the Ole Oak Tree"—Tony Orlando and Dawn, (2) "Bad, Bad Leroy Brown"—Jim Croce; and (3) "Killing Me Softly With His Song"—Roberta Flack.

Due to that strange miracle in Fort Leonard Wood, Missouri, I was entering the 11th grade, having been mysteriously promoted after failing the ninth grade. I had fallen back into a few of my previous patterns and behaviors, but one major change had occurred: I was no longer "dealing" or selling drugs. I had learned a big lesson regarding the consequences of that behavior.

Several other changes took place in the fall of 1973. On September 21st I got my driver's license. I had taken a driver's education class while in Missouri and easily passed the North Carolina driver's test. This provided me with an added level of independence and freedom, as long as my dad would loan me his white Maverick to drive.

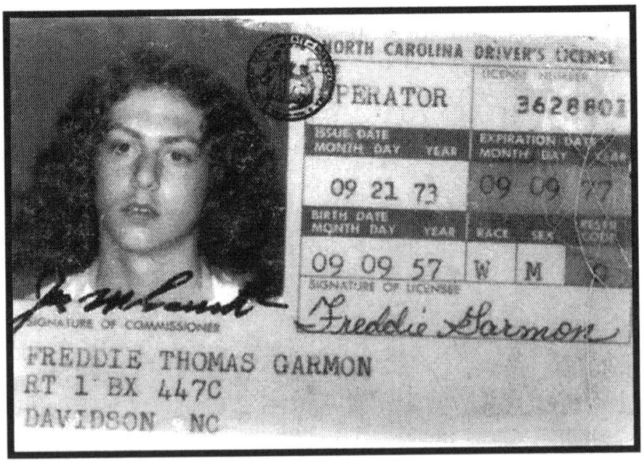

Anyone who belongs to Christ
has become a new person.
The old life is gone; a new life has begun!

2 Corinthians 5:17
New Living Translation

CHAPTER 10

Option B: CHANGE

During these first months back in North Carolina, a senior football player named Bobby Kiser befriended me and I started going to our high school football games to watch him play. I hung around after the games and rode around town with Bobby in his Mach I Mustang. Bobby had an older brother, Rick, who had graduated the year before and worked at the Cannon Mills factory.

The three of us soon became a team. This was good for me because neither one of these guys did drugs. They had grown up in church but smoked cigarettes, drank beer, and Bobby would smoke a little marijuana with me from time to time.

I distinctly remember the first time Bobby and Rick took me home to spend the night with them. It was a Friday night after a football game. We had spent time after the game riding in Bobby's car round and round a quarter-mile loop that included McDonald's as the main hangout. It was about 11:30 p.m. when we made our way to Bobby and Rick's house. We stood on the front porch ringing the doorbell till Bobby and Rick's mother, Deloris, came to let us in. She stood inside the screen door staring at me, asking, "Who is this? And what is he doing here?" Bobby began explaining who I was and that they wanted me to spend the night. I was allowed to stay, but I remember Bobby and Rick spending quite a bit of time in their parents' room that night explaining why they brought someone who looked like me home with them.

A month or so later Bobby invited me to watch a basketball game at our high school. I arrived early and, while waiting on Bobby to arrive, I watched the girls basketball team play the final 10 minutes of their game. I took special notice of a classmate on the basketball court. Carol Bennick was the point-guard, an exceptional athlete who had played this key position for our girls varsity team since her ninth-grade year (now in the 11th grade). Carol was not only an exceptional basketball player, she was a remarkable young lady—a prominent, influential Christian.

From that moment on, I had one goal: get to know Carol Bennick. In the days to come, I found opportunity while at school to be near Carol. I was smart enough to know I was barking up the wrong tree with a girl like this. Carol was from another culture, another level of society. She was the type of person I normally referred to as a "goody two-shoes," one that would never consider a guy like me.

Nevertheless, one day I found enough courage, with support from Bobby, Rick, and Carol's brother Chuck, to ask Carol out on a date. She quickly but tactfully turned me down. I remained persistent over the next few months but continually got the same disappointing result.

In December, during the Christmas break from school, I decided to make one more attempt with Carol. I asked if she would go out with me, and this time she answered, "Yes." But she qualified her positive response by saying that she would specify where we would go and what we would do. I agreed and was excited about it. Carol explained that her church youth group was having a Christmas party at her Sunday school teacher's home and that she wanted to go there. It sounded strange to me, but I wanted to be with her, so I agreed.

Friday night came and I picked up Carol in my dad's Maverick. We went to the party, and I remember feeling like an alien—a welcome alien, but an alien. Everything about this party was different from any party I'd ever attended. Especially strange to me was the part about devotions, prayer, and this thing they called "sharing." We ate holiday food, sang Christmas carols, and sat around in a big circle as 25 or more teenagers shared stories about their Christian faith. Later that evening as I took Carol home, I remember feeling as if I had visited some strange but mysteriously intriguing planet. This was all so new to me.

Our next date involved going to a late night New Year's party on New Year's Eve. I remember feeling pretty good about this second time out together, thinking that I must have behaved ok during the first date. I simply did not know how to behave around people like this. Not only did

I look like a drug-culture hippy, my language was habitually foul, and I was concerned something untoward would slip out accidently.

The late-night holiday party started at 10 p.m. at the home of another member from Carol's church. The plan was to leave the party at 11:30 p.m. and go to a local Episcopal Church where we would participate in a midnight Mass service. At the stroke of midnight, 1974 found me on my knees in that Episcopal Church. It wasn't anything personal. It was simply part of the religious ceremony connected to midnight Mass—kneeling on the padded kneeler attached to the back of each pew.

Interestingly enough, Carol took her time when it came to inviting me to attend an actual church service with her. I'm not sure if it was a conscious decision at the time, but it turned out to be a good strategy. Little by little Carol exposed me to another way of life without letting the experience be initially defined by a church service. I observed Christianity and people with a relationship to Jesus Christ from a safe distance before being placed in a full-blown Protestant/Pentecostal church-service setting. Incremental exposure was awkward enough; I'm not sure I could have withstood a frontal religious assault.

Three weeks after the New Year's party Carol invited me to church. That day, Sunday, January 20, 1974, started early. The Elm Street Church of God was a fairly large congregation, averaging approximately 500 regular attendees on any given Sunday morning. The church also had a good-sized youth group that primarily revolved around a youth choir that was extremely active, both inside the church and outside in the community. This particular morning the youth choir, of which Carol was a member, was singing at a local prison prior to the Sunday morning worship service. We met at the church fellowship hall at 6 a.m. for a breakfast and then went on to the prison. Sam Lumsden, youth director, and several other youth leaders cooked a huge breakfast. I was getting to know the teenagers in this group pretty good by now and was beginning to feel less awkward about being with them. I picked up Carol at 5:30 a.m., went to the breakfast, then we loaded the church vans for the short ride to the prison where they were singing. I remember my daddy commenting this had to be something or somebody special because I didn't get out of bed at 5:30 a.m. for anything.

The prison service was emotionally moving. Watching the teens—kids my age—singing about Jesus with such passion and enthusiasm was both challenging and inspiring. This was all so very different from anything I had experienced. Following the service, we made our way in the vans back to the church, arriving at 11 a.m. just in time for the morning worship service.

We jumped out of the vans and walked into a full sanctuary. The congregation was standing and singing the opening hymn. I really did not know what to expect and had not given it much thought. To me, it was simply another opportunity to be around Carol. Bobby and Rick Kiser also attended this church, so both were there as well, a reality that made me feel much better about being in an environment where I looked so different from everyone else. Remember, I had shoulder-length hair, an earring in my left ear, and only had blue jeans, t-shirts, and tennis shoes to wear. (In the 1970s, it was customary to dress up for Sunday morning church, men in suits and ladies in their finest dresses.) I guess you could say I stuck out like a sore thumb.

Three large groupings of pews in the church provided seating, with large aisles on the left and right sides of the large middle group of pews. I followed Carol as she made her way through the double doors in the back foyer and down the left side aisle to the third pew on our left. The row was full, so we had to slide by eight to 10 people to get to the other end of the pew, which happened to be against a wall with a stained-glass window. I sat against the wall with Carol sitting beside me to my right. I was now—like it or not—a captive of the situation. It would require real effort to get out.

A large choir of some fifty to sixty people were on the stage singing their hearts out. The emotion and enthusiasm in the room was obvious and contagious. The music being produced by the piano, organ, drums, and small group of horns was loud, and the entire congregation was in sync with everything the choir and instrumental ensemble were presenting. I remember being utterly amazed! This was so very unusual, but I liked it.

Everyone in the room was dressed nicely. It was evident they all had spent a significant amount of time getting ready for church and that they lived lives similar to those people I knew in Missouri. I didn't know life like this existed anywhere near where I lived. I just kept turning my head, looking around, from the front to the back. I couldn't decide whether I wanted to watch the people in the congregation or the people in the choir. The whole room was electric and mesmerizing. There was, however, one elderly lady, probably in her 80s, sitting on the front pew, right up against the aisle, who kept stealing my attention. This lady stood swaying side to side with the music, with her hands feebly raised into the air. I wasn't real sure why she was doing this, but many others, including Carol, were doing it too.

The choir, with director Eddy Wilson standing behind the pulpit facing the congregation, was leading the congregation through several songs in a red-backed hymnal. All the typical components of a Sunday morning church service, I would later learn, were part of that experience: singing, Scripture reading, an offering, and a special song. All this was prelude to the main course: the sermon. Pastor Don Anderson, a large, charismatic man with gray hair, preached a sermon with excitement and passion. I do not remember the subject of Pastor Anderson's sermon, but when he finished and asked for everyone to stand, a strange feeling came upon me.

The organist was playing, and Pastor Anderson was asking for people to make their way to the front of the stage for prayer. "Anyone who wants a new life in Christ, step forward," he invited. I immediately, yet unpredictably, found myself crying. I wasn't in pain. I wasn't afraid. I didn't know what this was. Along with my tears was an overwhelming draw to step out and move toward the front. I found myself vacillating between "do it" and "you'd be crazy to go down there." But before I knew what I was doing, I found myself reaching over with my right hand to signal Carol that I needed space to squeeze out behind her. I moved toward the aisle. This experience was surreal and dreamlike to me. I slid past the others on our row and into the aisle.

The next thing I remember is being on my knees, still crying, with my elbows on a long wooden altar that was wide enough for another person to be opposite me praying with their elbows on the altar as well. Several of these altars were placed at the front of the church between the first row of pews and the front of the stage. I didn't know what to pray. I wasn't even sure what this was about or why I had stepped out. I just knew that whatever these people had, I wanted it and that in response to my stepping out, something extraordinary and amazing was happening to me.

It was then that I felt hands touching my shoulders and arms. I started hearing voices surrounding me, voices that were also quivering with tears and praying with me. I looked up and around to see the entire youth choir and all the adult youth workers standing and kneeling all around me. I was surrounded by probably 50 people, most of whom were teenagers.

Suddenly I heard a deep voice speaking into my left ear. I had heard this voice before and it immediately brought a sense of momentary fear. I looked to my left to see a highway patrolman kneeling next to me. This man had pulled me or a friend I was with over numerous times during the past several years, and instead of arresting me, he talked to me (us). He tried to convince me there was more to life than what I was doing. I remember thinking he was off the wall. I was simply blind and could not comprehend at the time what he meant. On this occasion, however, he looked into my eyes and said very clearly, "Freddie, what we've tried to do for you over the past several years, the LORD has just done in a matter of moments." Again, I wasn't really sure what he was talking about, but it sounded really good.

We prayed there in the altars for quite a while, until finally most everyone had left the sanctuary except Carol, Bobby, and Pastor Anderson. I had never been hugged that much in my entire life! As we were leaving, I recall hearing Pastor Anderson say, "Remember, we have church again tonight at 6:30 p.m." As I moved down the aisle toward the back doors, I reached up and took my earring from my left ear. I never wore it again.

Driving home was an experience in itself, mostly because I couldn't stop crying. So much of something was coming out of me and much more of something else was happening inside of me that I could not contain.

Trying to Make Sense of It

Charles Finney (1792-1875) was an American Presbyterian minister and leader in the Second Great Awakening in the United States. He is often referred to as the Father of Modern Revivalism. On October 10, 1821, this 29-year-old lawyer decided he must settle the question of "his soul's salvation." Finney headed out into the woods determined to "give his heart to God or never come down again." After several hours, he returned to his office where he

"experienced such forceful emotion that he questioned those who could not testify to a similar encounter."

The Apostle Paul had a "Damascus Road" experience that so completely changed his life that he later indicated that his conversion experience was like becoming "a new creation" (2 Corinthians 5:17).

I am definitely not a Charles Finney, nor do I compare myself to Saint Paul, but I can testify to a Christian experience that miraculously and radically altered the framework, composition, and direction of my life. Can it be explained by nature, by nurture, or by inexplicable means? Nature caused me to be born into the sinful human condition. Nurture placed me inside the Garmon family and in an environment sabotaged to fail. But something incomprehensible and baffling happened on that special Sunday morning that produced a fundamental chasm between my life before and the life that would be lived afterward. I would, from time to time, experience ups and downs, great progress forward and lapses of faith that triggered great remorse. But from that day to this day, I never looked back. And the one and only variable that can possibly explain the change was the moment in time when I made a decision of the will to publicly believe.

Add to all this the fact that I had virtually no rational or biblical understanding concerning my conversion experience, but the passion ablaze inside me found its way out through almost every statement I made. And the kernel of hope ignited within me was growing every day. What's more, the passion was contagious, extremely infectious.

Carol's Perspective in Her Own Words

"I remember those first days when you noticed my basketball skills. I also remember you standing on the steps that led down to the locker rooms, shouting, "Go, #21!"

You never knew this, but Coach Edwards, being the strong overbearing coach that he was, had demanded that I not speak with you. "You were not my kind," he would say. I was only a babe in Christ myself, but I tried to listen to my Coach.

At the same time, the Holy Spirit was pulling on me to befriend you, and not hold you at a distance. Add to that the fact that my father was a sergeant on the police department, and had heard the name, "Freddie Garmon" before. He did not want me to spend any time with that "drug dealer."

I am confident that those prayers in your mother's closet had been heard, and nothing could stop them from coming to pass.... not even a tough basketball coach, nor a policeman father who would do anything to protect his "little girl." The power of a praying mother is nothing to mess with! She had wet your face with her tears and our Heavenly Father took notice. She would not be denied.

Another thing:

Your kindness to me—even while wearing those dirty jeans and white tee-shirts, far outweighed the other guys who wore all the right things, but God was not welcome in their lives. It goes to prove, that even young Christians, like I was then, who seek God earnestly, will be led by Him IF they only listen!

Fred, there is so much to say, and I know you have said it well in your book. I continue to be awed by the working of the Holy Spirit in the lives of those who want Him. Your story has been orally told by me for well over 38 years in the classes I have taught. I am overjoyed that it is now in this book."

Carol Bennick Bost
February 12, 2018

Carol Bennick and Freddie Garmon
1975

SECTION THREE

Self-monitoring is part of self-awareness, the absolute, number one, prerequisite for self-development.

CHAPTER 11

Inside Out

I arrived home that Sunday afternoon, walked into our mobile home, and said to my dad, "Daddy, I've been to church and I want to go get my hair cut." I don't remember ever seeing my daddy move that fast. He asked no questions and made no comments. He simply got up, found his keys, and said, "Let's go."

We made our way about 20 miles to my brother, J. F.'s home in Rockwell, North Carolina. J. F.'s wife, Betty Jo, was a beautician, so it made perfect sense to have her cut my hair, especially since it was Sunday. Daddy was smart enough not to say anything about waiting till Monday. He didn't want me to have any time to change my mind. Betty Jo cut it all off. Hair lay all over the floor around me. I walked away a clean-cut young man with my brother and sister-in-law standing in the doorway amazed.

It was nearly 6 p.m. when Daddy and I got home. All I could hear ringing in my ear was "church starts at 6:30 p.m." To Daddy's amazement, I wanted to go back to church. I arrived at church a few minutes late, once again finding them standing and singing. I went in this time on the right side and sat about two-thirds toward the back on the right-hand side. It came time for the sermon, and Pastor Anderson made his way to the pulpit. As he scanned the audience, his eyes stopped on me. He paused for what seemed to be an awkward minute or two, then said, "Freddie Garmon, is that you sitting back there?" I stood up and said a loud, "Yes, sir."

Now you have to understand the importance of this. I had never been one to draw attention to myself in a crowd. I had never spoken in front of a crowd. In fact, just the opposite. I had learned how to blend in and keep from being noticed. Standing up in a crowd like this was definitely out of character, and my actions surprised me.

Pastor Anderson then said, "Freddie, testify."

Now it's quite interesting to have unchurched people come to church. And one of the reasons it's interesting is because unchurched people do not understand a church culture's language. I had no idea what Pastor Anderson was asking me to do, but I felt like, from the context, he was asking me to come forward and talk. I stood up, walked down the aisle, up the three steps onto the platform, and found myself standing behind the pulpit. I felt as if everyone in the room was staring at me with their mouths hanging wide open. I had left church that very afternoon with long hair and an earring. I returned several hours later without the earring and with very short hair. I had sat in the back of the church and only Pastor Anderson, Carol, and Bobby had recognized who I was. Now here I was standing behind the pulpit, and everyone was waiting with bated breath to hear what I had to say.

My words were simple as I attempted to describe what had happened to me during the morning service. My simple words were, however, loaded with passion and heartfelt sincerity as I explained the struggle I experienced that morning, trying to decide whether or not to step out and come to the altar. I also tried to explain the interior stuff that was happening as I sensed emotions I couldn't control and did not want to control. And the more I talked, the more I cried, smiling at the same time. It wasn't long until people started moving toward the altar, especially the youth group. And the church found itself experiencing a jubilant time of celebration because someone who was "lost was now found." I guess you could say I had just preached my first sermon. I went home that night and for the first time knelt down beside my bed to pray. Alone in my room, I asked the LORD to guide my life and direct my steps.

I woke up the next morning excited about what this new day would bring. I rode to school with a friend who lived next door and had his own car. He asked me questions about what had happened to me all the way to school. Upon arrival at school I walked through the main foyer next to the administrative offices. I made my way to the cafeteria where everyone sat waiting on the first bell to ring—the bell signaling we were to go to our first morning "home room" class.

Normally a great deal of noise filled the hallways and cafeteria area during this morning time, and this day was no exception. What was different were the teachers and office workers coming out into the foyer and hallways to see me. I had been a person that brought a great deal of anxiety for school staff and now an obvious change had taken place. "What was going on?"

I walked into the cafeteria area and within less than a minute you could have heard a needle drop on the floor. Silence. Everyone was looking at me. "What happened to you?" was asked scores of times during this 11th-grade Monday in January 1974. And I answered the question by responding, "I went to church yesterday with Carol, and I got saved." My answer was mystifying to everyone but evidently convincing because every time I tried to answer and explain it, I would tear up and become very emotional.

By lunchtime I was inviting everyone to meet me at church that very evening (Monday night) at 6:30 p.m. to hear more about this astonishing experience that had changed my life. I'm not sure where this idea came from, but it seemed a logical next step considering all the interest and intrigue this most recent development was creating. Carol was concerned about my invitations and explained I couldn't just invite people to the church like that.

"We don't have church on Monday nights," she explained. "Pastor Anderson needs to give us permission." But it was done, and there was no stopping the evident momentum being generated. And while Carol was responsibly concerned, she was incredibly excited about what was happening in me and the influence it was having on our friends.

We arrived at the church that evening around 6 p.m. and already a large group of teenagers were standing in the front yard and around the church steps leading into the sanctuary. It didn't take long for Pastor Anderson to come around the corner to see what was going on. We explained what was happening and with a laugh or two, he unlocked the doors, turned on the lights, and gave approximately 60 young people run of the sanctuary. Carol and I kind of flew by the seat of our pants for the next 60 minutes or so, sharing our heartfelt commitment to Christ and His ability to change and direct our lives. This event, or one very similar to it, became a popular weekly occurrence for the next month or so. In fact, what happened in my life reverberated throughout the church, community and even into other congregations in the area to the point that I was contacted to speak at several youth meetings.

The next year and a half from January 1974 to May 1975 brought gargantuan changes to my life. Several components helped to stabilize my commitment to change and enabled me to stay the course:

- Weekly involvement with my local church
- Pastor Don Anderson's personal commitment to mentoring me
- My friendships with Carol Bennick and Bobby Kiser
- High school sports; *i.e.*, track, basketball, and football
- New friends at church and subsequently at school too
- Extracurricular activities at school (Thespian Society and academics)
- Speaking engagements for church youth groups.

High School Senior Year and First Family Member to Graduate

My senior year of high school was fun and exciting and fascinatingly different from anything I'd lived out prior to this time. I enjoyed a new friendship group, new hangouts, and new ways to occupy my time—a whole new culture. Looking back, several things helped me survive and make lifestyle changes successfully.

My leadership training describes a popular leadership model known as Situational Leadership. This particular model not only points out leadership styles (directing, coaching, supporting, delegating) but also the developmental levels of followers pertaining to every goal or task. These development levels are 1 enthusiastic beginner, 2 disillusioned learner,

3, capable but cautious performer, and 4, self-reliant achiever.[14] Nothing could describe better the development and changes taking place in my life during those first few months of this extremely different life I was living.

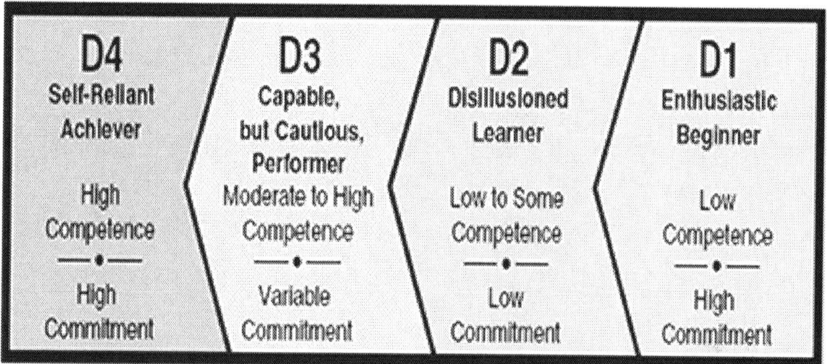

I hope you have been able to sense the joy, the relief, and the excitement I experienced during those first months of being a new Christian. According to Situational Leadership, I was at Developmental Level #1 (D1), the enthusiastic beginner stage. I was new to this entire culture, and it was exciting. I had fresh eyes. I was eager to learn, and my passion was easy to see and feel. I was also inexperienced and did not know what I did not know.

I quickly found myself tripping all over myself. In my previous environment, I had a pretty foul mouth. Granted, it probably wasn't as bad as others in my particular group, but cursing had been part of my accepted vocabulary and way of life. I didn't know how to communicate without using several decorative adjectives along the way. I did OK while I was "self-monitoring," —able to think about what I was doing, and actually censoring what I was saying.

Self-monitoring is part of self-awareness and is said to be "the absolute, number one, prerequisite for self-development." I had *never* in my life had a reason to be self-aware or to self-monitor, thus be self-disciplined about anything. I seemed to do well until something occurred that took my mind off the moment, like being surprised by something, good or bad. A few times, what came out of my mouth was nothing less than utterly embarrassing.

14 Ken Blanchard, Situational Leadership II. Developmental levels of followers.

I remember one occasion when Carol and I were on a date. Bobby Kiser and Carol's brother, Chuck, were in the back seat. A car unexpectedly pulled out in front of us, and I let a string of words pass across my lips that would shame a sailor. The silence in the car was inescapable, and I immediately realized the fool I had made of myself. I looked in the rear-view mirror to see Bobby and Chuck falling all over themselves laughing hysterically at me. But for Carol, there was nothing funny about what she had just witnessed. I apologized, but much damage had been done. Old habits die hard, and I learned that much of my past, while no longer visible on the surface, was still lying deceptively below the water line. I had come a long way, but I still had a very long way to go.

The Big Question

About this time in my story, people ask an obvious question: Did I marry Carol Bennick? Drum roll. . . . The answer is no. She was a heartbreak, but I survived and we have remained friends. Carol married a wonderful man from the Winston Salem, North Carolina, area named Tim Bost. They have lived a successful and influential life all these many years. I will, however, be forever thankful to Carol for stepping out of her comfort zone to befriend me.

A Disillusioned Learner

The next season of my life plunged me into what Situational Leadership[15] calls Developmental Level 2, or D2. It is the disillusioned learner stage and a developmental stage that is inevitable within any and every task or project we undertake. This stage is marked by inconsistency, confusion, discouragement, frustration, but still learning. Wow! A perfect definition!

Both research and experience tell us that this Developmental Level will be experienced many times in life and always represents a grand opportunity to learn that failure is a vital component in the learning and personal improvement process. In fact, leadership author John Maxwell wrote a book entitled *Failing Forward* where he describes this incredibly

---

15 Situational Leadership is model was developed by organizational psychologist Ken Blanchard. The SLII model is a research-based behavioral model that has been adopted by more than 30 million learners around the world. SLII's foundation lies in teaching leaders to diagnose the needs of an individual or a team and then use the appropriate leadership style to respond to the needs of that person or team—leveraging all the theory and design that has made SLII the world's most-taught leadership training model.

important principle. This is exactly what I was doing—failing forward and experiencing all the stuff that comes with that enlightening, sometimes embarrassing season. Here you have one or two choices: Learn from the experience or quit; go back to being who you were, doing what you were doing, or change.

Many people refer to this stage as the "sink or swim" stage. Others refer to it as the "survival of the fittest" or "rites of passage" stage. Call it what you will, it's tough. Some make it and others, well, they don't.

As I mentioned previously, we learn several ways: through experience, via mentors, through *mistakes*, and with formalized education. You will see that each of these pathways has played a major role in the drama of my developmental journey. Mistakes and/or failure may be the toughest to get a handle on.

Challenges administer a shock, instantly getting your attention. It's a jolt of uncertainty that carries a current of doubt; but with effort, discipline, and support, that doubt transforms into action and movement. Ultimately, if and when the challenge is conquered, a backward glance leaves the leader with confidence and insight that can be applied to the next challenge. It is in conquering difficult assignments such as these that people become ready to take on bigger challenges in life.

Most of the leadership that shapes our lives does not come from leaders with titles on an organization chart; it comes from leaders in our daily life-role relationships.

CHAPTER 12

Life-Role Leaders Save the Day

Contemporary evidence[16] suggests that the complex web of social relationships we experience, with family members, peers, and adults at school, exerts a much greater influence on our behavior than researchers had previously assumed.

This fact is ever so true in my life. At this intersection in my journey, several unsung heroes (life-role leaders) stepped in and stepped up. They will never in this life know the impact they had on me. Many of them have already passed, but their friendship, mentorship, and words of encouragement, at exactly the right place and time, helped me stay afloat long enough to get another breath and tread water just a little bit longer in the deep end of the pool. I would be wrong to not give honorable mention to a few of these "life-role" leaders who presently come to mind.

I was much too far out all my life
—and not waving but drowning—
"Not Waving But Drowning" poem by Stevie Smith

- *Bobby Kiser*, who became my best friend until his death several years after his high school graduation in 1974. Bobby broke his neck in

16 Harris, 2006.

a swimming accident and remained paralyzed until his death in October 1999. I still miss him. Bobby's circle of friends was very different from my typical running buddies, but it was Bobby who introduced me to a group of young men that still hold a place in my heart: Richard Brunson, Eddie McClure, Darryl Brock, and Randy Benton. Their influence still impacts me today. And Bobby's brother, *Rick*. We became even closer after Bobby's death, and Rick remains a close friend to this day.

- *Pastor Don Anderson.* The pastor of the Elm Street Church of God took me under his wing and became a surrogate father to me. The time he spent with me is difficult to understand today. I cannot put into words the impact Pastor Anderson had on me. His passing was another tragic blow. I still miss him.

- *Pam Adams.* Pam was the church secretary at the Elm Street Church of God in Kannapolis, North Carolina, when I started attending. She immediately began encouraging me and pouring into my life in an intentional way. Pam actually became as close to me as a blood sister. Pam passed away April 23, 2015. I miss her.

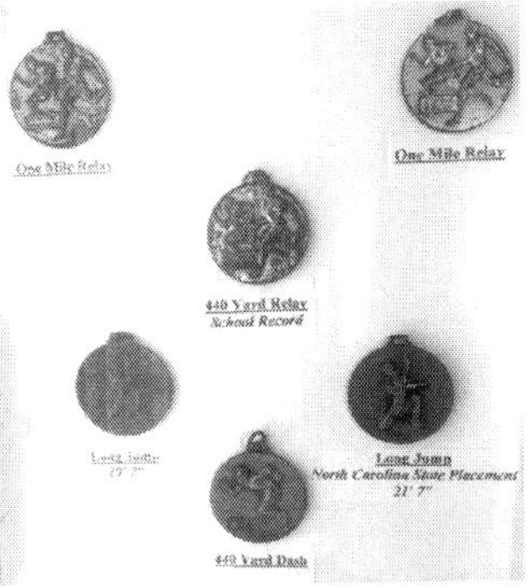

- *Coaches Shinn* (track), *Harwood* (football), and *Angley* (basketball) of Northwest Cabarrus High School in Concord, North Carolina. Make note here that I had never been involved in organized sports. My only experience with sports of any kind was that solitary basketball game in the sixth grade. All my high school athletic endeavors required learning from the bottom up. It's funny now, but I don't even remember these coaches' first names. We simply referred to them as "Coach."

  - *Coach Shinn* coached me two years in a row in my 11th- and 12th- grade years. Under his tutelage I earned six medals during our two Rocky River Conference state track meets. I won two silver medals for the one-mile relay, one silver medal for the 440-yard relay school record (Darryl Brock, Larry Rucker, myself, and Danny Kirkman, our anchorman—43 seconds), one bronze for the 440-yard dash (52 seconds), and two medals for the broad jump event—silver at 19' 7"and bronze for 21' 7". I was also awarded the "All Rocky River Conference" Award for an "All-Conference" time in the 220-yard dash at 23.1 seconds. It's funny and rather cheesy now, but I earned a nickname during those two years—"Fast Feet Freddie."

- *Coach Harwood* is remembered for several reasons. First, he was not our head coach; he was an assistant coach. Our head coach, Coach Ray, was a bulldog and extremely hard on his players. Coach Harwood was no softy, but he knew how to mix in just enough encouragement and praise to leave you with your self-esteem and the will to fight another day. I remember Coach Harwood coming to me after the last game of the season and saying, "Freddie, your competitive spirit and dogged determination to learn and not give up is exemplary. It has been a pleasure coaching you. Now go out there and make the basketball team too." Those words have never left me.

- *Coach Angley* was my Algebra teacher and my varsity basketball coach. I'm sure the only reason he kept me on the team was because Coach Harwood said I'd be a good cheerleader from the bench and a competitive practice dummy. I only played about 21 seconds that entire season, but we won the Rocky River Conference Championship and I learned to love basketball. It became an awesome hobby for me well into my 40s until my knees would no longer allow it. On Coach Angley's team I

learned the value of being a loyal team member, even if you were not a starter or primary player.

I lettered in all three sports and still to this day have dreams at night about what it would have been like to have played any or all of these sports earlier in my life, beginning in my junior high school years. I loved sports but simply did not have the experience needed to be a "starter" and excel in football or basketball. I was more successful in track due to the fact that it is more of an independent style sport, and I had two years' experience (junior and senior years). There is just no substitute for experience.

- *A high school guidance counselor*. Sadly, I don't remember her name, but her intervention into my life and her actions that involved getting me to think seriously about college were nothing short of inspirational. I remember our first conversation in her office at school. It was nearing graduation, and she was making sure I had all the required credit hours to graduate. In that first meeting, she planted a seed, a seed that initially got me thinking about "potential"—*my* potential. According to her, I could not possibly reach my potential unless I decided to continue my education. "But what am I supposed to do?" I asked her. In my mind, there was really no way I could go to college. First and foremost, I hadn't done very well with high school academics, so how in the world could I succeed at the college level? Second, money. College was expensive. Even community college seemed out of reach for me. And finally, remember that concept called culture? Remember, I said it possessed vortex-like strength to keep a person in his/her place. Three strikes and you're out.

High school sports kept me busy every day of the week during after-school hours. I was so tired when I got home that I usually ate my typical bologna and cheese sandwich with milk and went straight to bed. I was finally getting to bed in time to get the sleep I needed to get up early every morning. Even though my daddy had stopped drinking alcohol, he still wasn't much support in helping me manage my life. That was up to me. Sports became my great tutor, teaching me the discipline it takes to complete goals in life.

I was learning to stay busy, filling up every waking hour with respectable activities and valuable influences. I found time to add one more extracurricular activity to my senior-year schedule. I took a drama class and joined the Thespian Society.

We performed "The Wizard of Oz." I was the Scarecrow.

I guess the most quantifiable way to see that my life was truly changing in a substantive way was to look at my academic report card. The report card shown here was typical of my senior year classes. And as you can see, there was a remarkable change in the "Citizenship" category. I still had a little trouble with getting up and getting to school—time management issues—but I was doing much better.

1-14

CABARRUS COUNTY HIGH SCHOOL
Report Card

Northwest Cabarrus 1974-1975

STUDENT Freddie Harmon GRADE 12 B
HOMEROOM TEACHER [illegible] ROOM NO. 144
SUBJECT Algebra I CREDIT 1
TEACHER [illegible] ROOM NO. 226

PERIOD	1	2	Semester Exam	Semester Av.	3	4	Semester Exam	Semester Av.	Year
GRADE	78	80	75	78	80	84	—	82	80
CITIZENSHIP	A	A			A	A			
ABSENCES	1	3			1	4			
TARDIES	0	0			0	0			

MARKING CODE—A—93–100; B—85–92; C—78–84; D—70–77; F—Failure

Report of English and Social Studies

Teacher	Course Title	Grade

PARENT'S SIGNATURE
1 J. F. Harmon
2 J. F. Harmon
3 J. F. Harmon

Lonely Weekends and Friendships

Weekends were another story entirely. That is when this new life of mine got especially lonely. I had learned how to keep busy during the week, and I had casual friendships within my high school and church settings. The friends Bobby Kiser had introduced me to needed time to blossom. What was I supposed to do with myself on Friday and Saturday nights? What a dilemma! Old friends continually attempted to get me to hang out with them again, but I intuitively realized this was just not a good idea. Still, I did not have the kind of deep friendships necessary to have something to do and someone to do it with on weekends. Bobby Kiser provided a good outlet for a long time, but after his accident, I had no one.

I found myself sitting home many Friday and Saturday nights. In time, I developed appropriate friendships, but for six months to a year, I was a lonely young man on weekends.

Learning the Hard Way

Earlier I talked about the principle of "Failing Forward." During this season of my life, I learned one of my first and most vital lessons about making life change permanent.

Much of my former life easily dropped away on that special Sunday in 1974. I miraculously walked away from dysfunctional habits that take months and years to overcome. But there were other habits that were much harder to overcome, and I struggled with them for months, often in secret due to embarrassment. I walked away from smoking marijuana all at once and never had a serious temptation to do it again. But cigarettes were another story all together. I struggled with smoking cigarettes for at least two years. I was convinced smoking was wrong, but I enjoyed it and the addiction was hard to conquer. I did not believe then, nor do I believe now, that smoking in and of itself will condemn a person. I do, however, believe that such a terrible vice will damage your reputation, and we now know with scientific certainty that smoking will surely kill you. I once heard it said this way, "Smoking may not send you to hell, but it sure will cause you to smell like you've been there."

This represents another of those "obvious" things that people wrapped in a dysfunctional lifestyle just seem to miss. The smell from burning tobacco is one of those odors, similar to that of a skunk stench. The smells are different, but you can't seem to get it off of you. People who smoke become so accustomed to the smell that they don't smell it anymore—on their clothes, on their breath, in their car, or in their home. But everyone else smells it immediately. I can say with all honesty that quitting smoking was my most difficult dependency to break. I have tremendous sympathy for anyone trying to break an addiction.

During one of those lonely weekends, I finally gave in and made the choice to hang out again with some of my old buddies. They gladly came to get me and celebrated the possibility that "Freddie was back." I knew they would still be up to the same old dysfunctional activities, but I thought I was strong enough to resist and be the influencer now. How wrong I was! I found myself sitting in the backseat of a crowded car as marijuana was being passed from person to person. It didn't take long for me to give in to the peer pressure and join the crowd. Around 3 a.m. early that next morning, I found myself kneeling beside my bed to pray, which had become my nightly habit, feeling extreme remorse. I had given in to the temptation that involved wanting friendships more than I wanted to live a successful and healthy life. I learned from that night on how to be content staying at home until healthier relationships and opportunities presented themselves. This was a very good choice.

The bias of nature is always toward the wilderness, never toward the fruitful field.

A. W. Tozer

CHAPTER 13

The Bias of Nature

Shakespeare accentuates this principle and our propensities toward dysfunctional behaviors in Act 1, Scene 2, of *King Lear*:

The king falls from bias of nature. . . .

And then again in SCENE II, of *The Earl of Gloucester's castle*:

Thou, nature, art my goddess; to thy law, my services are bound.

Have you ever asked or been asked, "Why make your bed when you're going to sleep in it again? Do you get tired of taking out the trash or mowing the yard when you know you will have to do it again next week?"

A really big "aha moment" occurred for me years ago when preparing for a sermon. I came across this quote from A.W. Tozer:

> Every farmer knows the hunger of the wilderness, that hunger which no modern farm machinery, no improved agricultural methods, can ever quite destroy. No matter how well-prepared the soil, how well-kept the fences, how carefully painted the buildings, let the owner neglect for a while his prized and valued acres and they will revert again to the wild and be swallowed by the jungle or wasteland. . . .
>
> *The bias of nature is toward the wilderness, never toward the fruitful field* (italics mine).

In an instant, this fact meant more to me than a simple observation of interest to farmers; it was in fact a parable, an object lesson setting forth a law that runs through all aspects of life, affecting things spiritual as well as things material.

We cannot escape this law that persuades all things to remain wild or to return to a wild state after a period of cultivation. What is true of the field is true also of our lives, if we are but sensible enough to perceive it. The moral bent of nature is not toward order but away from it. And it would be well for each of us to learn this lesson a soon as possible. We sometimes leave the impression that it is possible to find at an altar of prayer some magic potion, counselor, or silver bullet. Something that, once and for all, would guarantee victorious living for the rest of our days. But this notion does not fit with reality.

A Lesson from Nature

The bias of our very nature is always toward the wilderness. It takes intentional, persistent effort to maintain a yard, a farm, a career, a ministry, a life. I personally learned a further lesson pertaining to this principle years later.

I love taking care of my lawn. My yard, especially my back yard, is my sanctuary. And it needs my undivided attention at least every four to five days; anything less and it will get away from me. The weeds, roots, moles, ants, vines, and chaos will literally cover any previous beauty and order that I've worked so hard to create. I found, however, that there were ways I could use the principle of "preventive maintenance" to help me with this struggle. I could do this each fall by using applications of "pre-emergent" fertilizer. This worked wonderfully for years until one year when I became so busy that I didn't have time to apply it. How I regretted this! I spent the entire next spring and summer trying to get rid of five or six different types of weeds. Hardly anything was left of my beautiful lawn that I had spent years cultivating. But major effort and persistence allowed me to once again get on top of it, and I determined to never let this happen again.

Mistakes and failures in life *will* happen. It is not *if* we fail, fall, or make a mistake, it's *when*. We all need grace, mercy, forgiveness, and understanding at some time in our lives. We must always remember and determine to never allow these propensities to disqualify us. As the Apostle Paul said in 2 Corinthians 4:9, "I may be knocked down, but I'm never knocked out" (*paraphrased*).

Then again Paul mentions the following:

> I want to do what is right, but I can't. I want to do what is good, but I don't. I don't want to do what is wrong, but I do it anyway. . . . I have discovered this principle of life—that when I want to do what is right, I inevitably do what is wrong (Romans 7:15-20, *paraphrased*).

High School Graduation and the Water We Swim In

I was nearing the end of my high school journey and getting excited about being the only person in my entire family to graduate from high school. Icing was added to the cake when my classmates voted me as "Friendliest." Oddly enough, the girl selected was Becky Garmon, Principal Robert Garmon's daughter. He would want me to be sure you understand that we are of no relation.

A cheerful personality, a pleasant smile and their willingness to always help out were the determining factors which won Becky and Freddie Garmon title of "Friendliest."

Becky was President of the Art club and active in the FHA and Jr Boosters' Club.She served as an officer of her class for 2 years.

Freddie was an active member of the Thespian Society and Monogram Club. He was very versatile in sports, being active on the varsity football, basketball, and track teams.

This was quite a turnaround! Just two years before, I had been expelled from school for dealing drugs.

I graduated in May 1975. It was one of the proudest days of my life. And even though no one from my family attended, I knew they were proud of me.

Attending events like this just wasn't part of our culture. They simply didn't feel like they fit with such crowds. This type of response is not that uncommon in low-income families. One study found that only 36 percent of low-income parents were involved in school activities on a regular basis. This is compared with 59 percent of parents above the poverty line.[17] Take note, it is not always correct to assume these are bad or heartless family members. The feelings and constraints of inferiority run deep and are often reinforced by conscious and unconscious behaviors of the crowd.

We don't think about or talk much about class consciousness or culture, but it *is* important and influential. Culture is said to be like a vortex, a whirling mass of water where a suctioning force operates. Culture is also often likened to centrifugal force, pulling together disparate or incongruent groups who share a common enemy. Upper-crust society was that common enemy for us. I grew up unconsciously thinking that my culture or way of living was the only way of living. I have since learned that there's far more behind cultural indifference and dysfunctional behavior. It cannot be simply dismissed as "lower-class" issues. For those living in it on a day-to-day basis, it is not an aberration. It is *the water they swim in.*

The most obvious important realities are often the ones hardest to see. And so it is with this thing we call culture. I had lived 16 years in one type of culture (water), and now I was living in a completely different culture (water). Jesus himself told His disciples that they would become "fishers of men" (Matthew 4:18-22). Fishermen pull fish out of one environment and place them in another. Is this not what happened to me?

I Didn't Choose This Life, Yet I Live It

I once read a poem that describes the experience of pain, loss, poverty, and dysfunctional family life. The poem can symbolize many things, but its official title is "Bondage of Poverty."

> I didn't choose this life yet I live it
> Every day I face my woe
> A life of which I have no control
> I've heard of people who live happy
> With three or maybe four square meals a day
> I've heard of people who drive for miles
> Who never get tired from the beating of the midday.

17 U.S. Department of Health and Human Services, 2000.

I heard of a place where water flows free and clean
I have heard of places where people smile
I lost my will, so long ago.

I didn't choose this life yet I live it
Every day I face my woe
My life runs out of control
I know there are places where people hear your cries
Places where you could sleep and rest for a little over an hour or more
There are schools where the teachers teach
And the students truly learn
I know there are places, though I've never seen
Where living happy...is completely free
But to me it's all a dream.

I didn't choose this life and now I refuse to live it
Every day I challenge my woes
I must gain control
My lack shall not be the limit but the means to flourish
If someone just like me can live free
Why can't I?
I will look at my life and smile, and love the simple things
Cause someday I know, I'll look back and say
"Those were great things"
I will take a chance to smile and I know it won't hurt
I will will myself to be free
From this bondage of poverty. (Samuel, United Kingdom)

This idea of "being out of control" beautifully depicts the way I felt after my mother passed away. I vividly remember crying and asking God as a 9-year-old little boy, "Why?" "Why did You allow this to happen to me?" And from that time on that little boy was cast into a life that can truly be best described as "out of control."

It is terrifying to sense you're standing at the edge of an abyss with nowhere to turn to for help and no one to hear your cries for help. Every day was an endless attempt to survive. Before my mother's death, she took care of everything, but suddenly she was gone, and everything changed. Nourishing meals, three times a day, were gone. Bedtime routines were gone. Having something decent to wear and knowing what to wear were gone. What replaced all this was insecurity at a deep psychological and actual level. Such was my reality for years —through no cause of my own, I had to become the sovereign and self-determining manager of my life. Not at 18 or 21 years of age but at 9 years old. And I was scared to death. But what can a

9-year-old boy do? You learn to live a haphazard life, wandering to and fro, here and there, doing whatever you must at the moment to survive.

Spare Change

I hardly ever share this next part of my high school experience. I choose to share it here for what I hope will be obvious reasons. Prior to my conversion experience, I learned to meet my needs in dysfunctional ways. Mostly I sold drugs, played pool, gambled, and ran with people who did the same things. In this way we had money to get the things we needed. What we needed was never extravagant. It was always just enough to get by—food, some meager clothes to wear, and gasoline for whosever vehicle we were lucky enough to get around in.

After my conversion, my financial situation changed quite a bit. Selling drugs and playing pool had kept money in my pockets. We still lived in a single-wide mobile home deep in the countryside. We still lived on my and Daddy's Social Security checks and whatever income my sister JoAnn could muster up from her drapery business. I did well every day to have enough money to get the school cafeteria lunch that was provided at that time for about 45 cents. A carton of milk was five cents extra. My life was changing for the better, but no longer having an income stream was a difficult adjustment.

I evidently had no pride at all because I went around every day at school after eating my lunch asking friends if I could have the "spare change" left on their tray. It was typically five to 10 cents, sometimes as much as 50 cents, and most of them would let me have it. I could get between a dollar or two every day doing this. By Friday I usually had enough money to get a quarter-pounder meal at McDonald's. This was especially important because McDonald's was the primary hangout on Friday and Saturday nights. We had a circle in Kannapolis and one in Concord where everyone drove their cars around and around, usually after a meal at McDonald's. Understand this. I was hungry. It was awesome to be able to have something to eat other than school cafeteria food and bologna-and-cheese sandwiches. But the primary reason I wanted the money was to be like everyone else. Without that couple dollars earned from basically begging for spare change every day, I would have to sit at McDonald's with my friends and watch them eat or just not go. Not going was not an option.

What Came Next?

Life was going along fairly well except for the fact that I was beginning to grow cold in my Christian faith. The rigorous and organized schedule I had submerged myself in during high school had ended and now I had the task of finding something to do with my timef. And, yes, that magnet of temptation still reached out to my dysfunctional past.

Graduation had been a wonderful marker in my life, but it brought with it major anxieties. My meager Social Security check was supposed to keep coming until I graduated from high school and/or was 18 years old, and turning 18 was just a little over three months away. What was I going to do? It may not seem like much to you, but the unnerving panic was real to me.

The third stanza in "Bondage of Poverty" is the important and empowering paragraph for me. I get inspired still to this day every time I read it. It reveals a determination to change. An intentional choice to do something different to achieve a different outcome. To finally realize there may be a lot of things in this life that I'm powerless to change and/or control, but there are many other things that, with a little effort, I can control. If other people I see can live lives that are happy and healthy, then so can I.

I believe that *kernel of hope* mentioned before was ignited in me, awakening this reality and empowering me with the knowledge that life could be different, that I did not have to live stuck in an endless cycle of dysfunction. With God's help, I could will myself to be free from that cyclical and sucking vortex.

> I didn't choose this life and now I refuse to live it
> Every day I challenge my woes
> I must gain control
> My lack shall not be the limit
> but the means to flourish
> If someone just like me can live free
> Why can't I?
> I will look at my life and smile, and love the simple things
> Cause someday I know, I'll look back and say
> "Those were great things"
> I will take a chance to smile and I know it won't hurt
> I will *will* myself to be free
> From this bondage of poverty.

So, as the colloquial saying declares, I put on my big boy pants and stopped whining. I chose to start believing more in the possibilities of my future than in the "assumed constraints"[18] of my past. I'm not sure I have or ever will completely be free of all the "stuff" of my past. I am aware of and now realize that a few assumed constraints, as hard as I try, may always be with me. They are entrenched deep inside a 9-year-old boy that I still care for. That little boy and his pain still represent "pearls of great price" that remain part of a precious, nevertheless, painful and lonely past.

I did find a consoling passage, however, in Scripture that seems to address just such a circumstance like this. In 2 Corinthians 12:8-10 the Apostle Paul said,

> Three different times I begged the Lord to take it away. Each time he said, "My grace is all you need. My power works best in weakness." So now I am glad to boast about my weaknesses, so that the power of Christ can work through me. That's why I take pleasure in my weaknesses, and in the insults, hardships, persecutions, and troubles that I suffer for Christ. For when I am weak, then I am strong (*NLT*).

The Decision to Move Onward and Upward

I went to work after high school graduation at a Western Sizzlin Steakhouse on Highway 29 between Kannapolis and Concord, North Carolina. With the assistance of my high school guidance counselor, I applied for and received a "Basic Educational Opportunity Grant" (BEOG) from the U.S. Government. The BEOG assisted with my tuition costs.

In September 1975, I turned 18 and enrolled at Central Piedmont Community College (CPCC) in downtown Charlotte. I had witnessed first-hand just how tough and difficult the job of a brick mason was, so I knew I didn't want to follow in the footsteps of my dad and brothers. Construction, though, was the only trade I knew anything at all about. From that, I decided to try what I reasoned to be an easier route. I took

18 An "assumed constraint" is a belief based on past experience that limits current and future experiences. The healthy advice encourages one to "challenge" these limiting beliefs. For example, a baby elephant has a wooden stake and rope tied to its leg to hold him/her in place. As the elephant grows larger and older, he or she "assumes" the stake and rope still holds them. In addition, for many years it was widely believed that human beings could not run a mile in less than four minutes. On May 6, 1954, in Oxford, England, Roger Bannister ran the mile in three minutes, 59 seconds. Forty-six days later John Landy broke the record. In 1957, 16 more runners broke the record. Today, over a thousand people have run the mile in less than four minutes, including high school athletes.

classes to become an architect and/or interior designer. My experience with construction and my artistic abilities seemed to point me in that general direction.

My daddy could not afford to help me much, but when he heard I had really been accepted to community college, he took me to purchase my very first car. He paid $500 for a white 1966 Plymouth that became my pride, joy, and only mode of transportation for the next foreseeable future. It was a wonderful and emotionally moving gesture on my dad's part. I miss him.

Tragedy and a Reality Check

Leaving high school took me away from the day-to-day relationships and influences of close Christian friends. It wasn't long till I started struggling again with old habits and the temptation to see my old buddies. I mentioned before that cigarettes were my primary nemesis, and I quickly found myself smoking again. I was flirting around with old friends again too but had enough sense to keep myself from certain settings.

I remember well the day Bobby Kiser's brother, Rick, called me and told me that Bobby had an accident while swimming. Bobby had been dating our high school principal's daughter and spent many weekends at their lake property swimming. On this particular day Bobby dove into the same river, in the same place he'd dove many times, but this time his head struck the bottom of the lake and broke his neck, permanently damaging his spinal cord and paralyzing him from his neck down. This news shook me to my core and caused me to reevaluate every aspect of life.

A few days later I visited Bobby in the hospital. The sight of him in that hospital bed, with screws in his head and neck, was almost more than I could stand. I don't remember making a conscious decision to recommit myself to living a good life, but I know that from that time on, there was no more ambiguity about the direction of my life. Once again, I experienced a tragedy that would serve to alter my life. I guess you could say this tragedy forced me to realize that none of us are bulletproof or immortal. It also started my intentional search for meaning in life, the quest to make a difference.

"The harder I worked, the luckier I got."

Oxford Dictionary of Quotations
A proverb that dates to the late 16th century

CHAPTER 14

A Still Small Voice

In spite of all my ups and downs, I continued to share my story about my transformed life everywhere I could. I tried to stay busy doing productive things, which primarily consisted of working and going to community college. One day in mid-October 1975, I was sitting in the Central Piedmont College library studying, looking out the huge windows at the downtown Charlotte cityscape. From out of nowhere came a thought: *You need to go to Lee College and study to be a minister.* I must have sat there contemplating this idea for an hour or more. I concluded that it was impossible. Lee College was a private Church of God college that brought with it hefty expenses. It was a dream, but it simply wasn't for me.

I had grown up in a poor culture. Compared to those I had met in church, I had grown up in an unsuccessful culture as well. Consequently, I had developed deep feelings of inferiority and inadequacy. I had fallen into the mental trap of assuming that people who were doing better than me were actually better than me. Eventually, though, I learned this was not necessarily true. They were just doing things differently and what they had learned to do, within reason, I could learn as well. But it was a while yet before I consciously became aware of this amazing new discovery.

The next Friday night I found myself speaking at a local Baptist Church youth event. I did my typical talk about how a kernel of hope had radically changed my life, led the youth group in prayer, and then started spending time talking and playing board games with those in attendance.

I had noticed while I was speaking a well-groomed gentleman standing in the back of the fellowship hall. He listened to what I had to say with focused attention. I had intuitively learned to find several people throughout an audience who provided encouragement through their facial expressions and eye contact. This man was the epitome of that idea; he was genuinely interested. It wasn't long before he made his way over to me and asked if he could talk with me.

The man gave me his business card and introduced himself, explaining that he was with the "Ford Foundation," a foundation representing a Christian philanthropist. He then cut straight to the point and asked if I had any plans to continue my education. I explained that I was presently attending community college and where I thought my present plans might take me. He then asked if I had ever considered going into the ministry. I replied, "In fact, I thought about it earlier this week, but I quickly dismissed it due to the financial restraints of such a dream." The man quickly replied, saying, "I wouldn't dismiss it so quickly, young man." His guarantee to me was that if Lee College, a Christian institution, would accept me, then the Ford Foundation would cover all my tuition, room and board as long as I maintained passing grades. I was blown away. How could this be? I was ecstatic!

The next month Randy Benton, Richard Brunson, and I made the six-and-a-half-hour trip to Cleveland, Tennessee, to visit Lee College during their annual Homecoming weekend. We were such naïve guys and didn't know anything about how to get there. What was supposed to take six-and-a-half hours took us more like 10 hours after getting lost several times.

I remember standing and praying that first night in the window of our room at the Holiday Inn. I acknowledged just how unbelievable it was that I was even thinking about this, let alone standing on the verge of actually making such a decision. I was moving forward with such simple faith.

The next two days were like heaven on earth to me. The Lee College campus was beautiful. Teenagers and young adults from all over the United States and from several foreign countries attended. Families, along with prospective students, added to the festive atmosphere. My friend Carol was there. Gary Sheets, another young man from my home church was there, along with several other people from Kannapolis and Concord. All of this worked together to create an aspiration that could not have been any more dreamlike and desirable.

I worked that weekend with counselors and financial advisers. We transferred my BEOG grant from Central Piedmont Community College to Lee College, and I gave them a letter of intent from the Ford Foundation. My grades were nowhere near what I needed for proper admittance into college, but they allowed me to register for admission and work toward acceptance as a probationary student. We made our way back home, this time arriving in a little over six hours.

I spent the next few weeks anxiously waiting on news from Lee College. Would I actually be accepted? Finally, the day came and I opened the letter. I had been accepted under academic probationary status. My first and second semester would have to meet their academic criteria.

Getting accepted into college led me to have some unbelievable conversations. Conversations with my daddy and other family members who just could not imagine a member of the Garmon family in college. Conversations with Pastor Don Anderson and other trusted Christian friends. Conversations with friends from my past, friends who were simply inquisitive and wanted to hear more about what had happened to cause this change in me.

I was only a few weeks away from leaving home and walking from the Land of Familiar into the Land of the Unknown. My anxiety level was high, but my excitement level was helping to maintain a healthy equilibrium. Still several remaining flies were spoiling the ointment of this new college adventure. First, I was "leaving my daddy." Daddy was old, he was lonely, and his emphysema caused by cigarette smoking was getting dreadfully worse. I did not want to leave him.

My daddy and I had what could be described as an unusual relationship. Daddy was a construction man and epitomized every aspect of what you think of when you think of a construction worker from that generation. It was all he had ever known since he quit school in the third grade. The skill of brickwork had enabled him to support a wife and raise eight children. I was the lucky eighth.

Daddy was thus a hard man. A drinking man. A cussing man. But a good man. I don't remember my daddy ever raising his voice to my mama. He loved the ground she walked on. I don't remember my daddy ever being mean to anyone. He always had a labor crew, many of whom were African-American workers and most of whom were like family to us. I vividly remember one man called J.P. He was a black man who had worked with Daddy forever. I don't remember a time when J.P. didn't work for Daddy, and Daddy treated him and every other laborer, white or black, with dignity and respect. This was in a time (1960s) when there just wasn't a great deal of dignity or respect given to black Americans.

Daddy was a tough man, but he loved me. Those words were never actually spoken to me while I was growing up, but I knew that he loved me. In fact, there was *never* a day that I doubted Daddy's love. Even during that terrible grief-filled time of drunken stupors and absentee days, I knew he loved me.

Shortly after Bobby Kiser's accident, I began contemplating life without my daddy. This is actually a principle taught by the late Stephen Covey: "Begin with the end in mind." I knew nothing of this principle at that time, but somehow, probably a result of previous loss and pain, I knew intuitively that if valuable words were to be spoken to those you love, they should be spoken now.

I thought for days about saying those words to my daddy, but I just couldn't bring myself to speak them. Finally, one Sunday afternoon I came home from church and saw Daddy sitting in his favorite green chair watching a Sunday afternoon Western. I knelt down beside his chair—he seemed startled—looked him in the eyes and said, "Daddy, I love you." It seemed like an eternity, but then came the words from his mouth, "Son, you know I love you too." Nothing more was said; there was no need to prolong this awkward but wonderful moment any longer. I stood up and walked away, triumphantly saying to myself, *Yes, yes, yes!* That was the first of many times we would share those words from that time on. How could I leave him?

The second fly in the ointment that was spoiling my college excitement was the worry about not having proper clothes to wear. —Enter Connie and Richard Britt. The Britts had young children in the youth group at the Elm Street Church of God and therefore had a front-row seat to my transformational journey. I never told anyone about my clothing need and anxieties, but one day out of nowhere Connie Britt came to me and asked if I'd like to work for them at their clothing store during the Christmas holidays. The timing could not be more perfect! School and working at

Western Sizzlin occupied my weekdays that December, and working at the clothing store occupied my weekends. I earned enough money at the clothing store and, along with the huge discount given by the Britts, was able to buy some "awesome threads." I was ready for college. And I learned something important about myself—I was a fairly good salesman, earning "top salesman" at their store that Christmas season.

A Step Into the Unknown

It was January 1976, and my sister JoAnn had fixed sausage biscuits with cheese for breakfast. Gary Sheets pulled into our country dirt-road driveway to take me a world away to Lee College. At that moment a nobody named Ordinary, who lived in the Land of Familiar, took a deep breath, got in Gary's car, and stepped outside his comfort zone. Daddy and JoAnn were standing on the small front porch of our single-wide mobile home as we pulled away. Down that old dirt road we went.

An Unexpected Visitor

I entered my freshman year at Lee College in January of 1976. Most dorm rooms were full, but one room happened to be available in the nicest boys dorm on campus, Hughes Hall. I moved onto the second floor with another guy who, coincidently, was just arriving at Lee too. Roger Armstrong was coming out of the military and was placed in Hughes with me. We became roommates and good friends.

Bill George

Several weeks into the semester, what would turn out to be a life-altering relationship began. I had been playing basketball all afternoon one Saturday and had returned to the dorm, taken a shower, and was standing at the sink in my room shaving. My room door was standing open to the hallway. Suddenly, standing in my doorway was my new testament professor, Dr. Bill George. "Hi, Fred. I hope I'm not dropping by at a bad time."

I hurriedly wiped the shaving cream from my face and grabbed a shirt. "No, sir. It's not a bad time at all. I'm glad to see you. Come on in."

Dr. George responded, "I don't need to come in, but I'd like to know if you've got time to go to Gondolier and have a cup of coffee?" My answer was quick, "Yes, sir. Let me get my shoes on."

The relationship, mentorship, and ultimate friendship that started that day over a cup of coffee lasted 41 years.

Dr. George was an incredible teacher. He taught Old and New Testament Survey and so many students enrolled in his classes that he had to use the campus auditorium and take roll by assigning numbers and calling out the numbers at the beginning of each class. Dr. George taught at Lee College for several years before taking a position as pastor of the Dauphin Island Parkway Church of God located just outside Mobile, Alabama.

A Letdown and a Lesson

Midway through my first semester at Lee College (March 1976), all seemed to be going well. I was making new friends, getting overwhelmed by extracurricular college activities, learning to go to class, and studying. I remember going to the campus mailroom one morning and actually finding a piece of mail in my mailbox.

In 1976 we had no computers. We wrote our research papers and assignments by using a typewriter; the cutting-edge technology was "correction tape." There were no cell phones. The only way I could call home, which I seldom did, was to use the public pay phone located midway on my dorm-room floor. So letters were important. I opened the letter while walking to a campus chapel service. The timing became significant because I was going to need a faith-inspiring message after reading that letter. I opened the envelope, and the letterhead immediately let me know it was from the Ford Foundation. It was short and to the point:

> Brother Fred,
>
> I regret that our foundation will not be able to fund your college tuition. We were not aware that the college you chose to attend was a Pentecostal institution. Our funding criteria prevents funding such institutions.
>
> Respectfully. . . .

I immediately started to panic. *What was I going to do? How could I possibly afford this school now? How could this be happening?* A dark fog of pessimism and negativity threatened to move in.

I have, however, always seemed to rebound from adversity, difficulty, and misfortune rather quickly. I possessed an outlook on life, especially after my conversion, that leaned toward seeing the world through a glass half-full rather than one that was half-empty. That kernel of hope always seemed to win the day.

Early on I explained that *hope* consists of *agency* and *pathways*. Simply put: hope involves the will to get there and figuring out different ways to do it. That seemingly insignificant kernel of hope was now empowering me (agency, motivation) with a mindset and a strategy that would move me forward toward finding a way (a pathway) to stay in school and pay for my college education.

It is so easy to worry ourselves sick. In fact, it is one of the default responses hardwired into our human experience. Nevertheless, over and over in Scripture we read the words, "Don't worry." But you and I both know, if we're honest, that it's easier said than done. Still, *it can* be done.

I once read, while studying *How to Win Friends and Influence People*, what Dale Carnegie had to say about worry. He taught tactics and simple exercises that truly help put worry in its proper place. In fact, he wrote another book about it titled *How to Stop Worrying and Start Living*. Carnegie explained that "over 90% of the things we worry about never happen." Consult the law of averages. The law of averages refers to the probability of a specific event occurring. Chances are good that whatever you're worried about isn't likely to happen.

Worrying, it has been said, is as useless as punching yourself in the face. Worrying doesn't help you. In fact, it does nothing. We share our worries with other people and often create an echo chamber of worry and fear. We have to pull ourselves together and do something.

I left chapel that day, talking to myself: *Be patient and think. Be patient and think.* By the end of the day, I knew what I had to do: *Have courage, trust the simple faith that got you to where you are, and get another job.*

More Hope, Another Lesson Learned

I had my BEOG grant from the U.S. Government. I had learned that I would continue to receive my Social Security check from my daddy's disability until I was 22 or until I graduated from college. This, along with the Ford Foundation scholarship, would have been the ticket. But now half my financial plan was gone.

By the end of the week, I got a job washing dishes every afternoon in the college cafeteria. I went to work Tuesday and Thursday nights at the local Cosmopolitan Spa on Keith Street, and I worked more aggressively to secure speaking engagements on weekends at nearby churches and youth groups. I even worked for an office cleaning company as an "on-call" employee, working for them every chance I could. I had a plan. Now I had to find a way to consistently implement my plan, a way to execute the plan for the next three and a half years.

When You Have Done All You Can

I wish I could tell you that all was smooth financial sailing during the next several years, but life is just not that way, is it? I made it to the end of my first semester and was close to having paid my entire bill. A week before the end of the semester and final exams, I went again to the mailroom. In my box I found a notice from the registrar's office explaining that I owed $750 and that this amount had to be paid in full before I could take my exams. It was Wednesday and final exams were scheduled to begin that next Monday.

That fog of gloom and doom was once again present just over the horizon, but I remember going back to my dorm room and doing all I could do at that time. I had brought an old green faux-leather recliner from home. It served a triple purpose as a great chair to study, to take a good afternoon nap, and to kneel and pray. I knelt to pray. I knew I had done all I could do. I could not work any harder, study any more faithfully, trust any more sincerely, or contact anyone that could help. I got up from prayer knowing all I could do now was rest.

The next day and a half I just went about my business doing what I did every day: going to class, going to work, going to the library to study. On Friday morning, the last full day of the semester, I went one last time to the mailroom. I found a solitary envelope. I looked at the return address but did not recognize the names handwritten there. I did, however, recognize the city of its origin—Charlotte, North Carolina, my hometown. What I read when I opened the envelope was nothing less than mind-blowing!

Several months earlier I had conducted a weekend speaking engagement (youth revival) at a small Foursquare Church that my sister Nancy

Cunningham attended. I did not know that two elderly ladies were inspired to have several yard sales to raise money for my college tuition. Once they had done all they could do, they sent their check to me. It arrived the very last day it could have arrived. The check was for $780. Their generous act of kindness had raised just enough money for me to pay my tuition bill, buy a tank of gas for my '66 Plymouth, and get a quarter-pounder meal at McDonald's in Black Mountain on the way home for summer break.

That Monday I took my final exams, barely made it past academic probation with a 1.7 semester grade-point-average[19], and left Cleveland, Tennessee, for home. A 1.7 GPA was not much to be excited about ... normally. But I was not your "normal" student. A 1.7 GPA was actually pretty good considering where I had come from.

The lesson I walked away with from that first semester of college was this: "The harder I worked, the luckier I got."

19 1.7 GPA out of a possible 4.0 GPA. Grade Point Average (GPA) is the process of applying standardized measurements of varying levels of achievement in an academic course of study; *i.e.*, a 3.7 GPA is an A- whereas a 4.0 GPA is a solid A.

Your journey is not over when you fall.
It's over when you stop getting up.

CHAPTER 15

My Spiritual Desert

I drove the six-hour trip home and spent that summer working for my brother J.F., who was doing brick work for Pastor Don Anderson. The church was building the Big Elm Nursing Home, and I worked that summer as a labor hand, carrying brick, making cement, and building scaffolding. That summer break seemed to drag by. I missed my new friends and the complete campus culture that surrounded Lee College.

I was, however, also struggling with a new and hard-to-deal-with experience. I explained earlier just how mysterious and wonderful my conversion experience was. This euphoric experience had been with me for a long time and had become my new normal. It's rather difficult to explain this exhilarating sensation. It's like someone crammed you full of optimism, hope, and enthusiasm.

But one morning I woke up and it was gone. It was like black and white. I immediately recognized the difference. It was as if someone had drained it while I slept. *What was up? What was wrong? Had I done something to cause this amazing reality to go away?*

The real test came at church that next weekend. Whatever this was inside me had always become activated, stimulated, and triggered in a church service. But now? Nothing. Just a dry and empty sort of feeling. Boy, this was different! I spent my summer months wrestling with this new funk in which I found myself. I tried to keep a good attitude and somehow find a way to get "that"—whatever "that" was—back. I sought counsel from everyone I could—Pastor Anderson, Pam Adams, Rick Kiser, youth director Sam Lumston, and friends in the youth group. Nothing seemed to help.

I spent that summer and the next semester at college (fall 1977) experiencing what I now call the *desert drought of the soul.* I had, by default, connected that feeling-experience with what I thought to be "the presence of God." I told everyone that I just couldn't "feel" God anymore. I knew I had done nothing sinful or shameful to cause the Lord to leave me. So why was this happening? Day after day. Week after week. Month after month.

"Oh God, you are my God, earnestly I seek you ... in a dry and weary land where there is no water" (Psalm 63:1, *NIV*).

Evidently I was not alone in this experience. The passage above makes it clear that King David also experienced something similar to what I referred to as "a desert." Do you ever feel that way? We all go through seasons when life seems dry and barren. Nevertheless, the Bible is filled with hope and promise that God will bring you through the drought of the soul. I just hadn't learned this lesson yet.

The 16th-century mystic John of the Cross referred to this season of spiritual dryness as "the dark night of the soul" during which it seemed as though God was no longer there. This season is especially difficult for people like me who, prior to, had walked in an almost continual awareness of God's presence. But suddenly, nothing.

It is during this "dark night" I realized that, on our path to spiritual maturity, we don't go from mountaintop to mountaintop. We have to walk through a few valleys as well. It is not just the spiritual life. It is life. Period.

This "dark night" experience is like being on a roller coaster. One day you're up. One day you're down. If you wake up feeling good, then you feel saved. If you wake up feeling down, then you feel lost. In the drug world, we would do what is called a "goof ball"—taking two types of drugs, an upper and a downer, at the same time. It is extremely dangerous. Don't ask the obvious question: *Why would anyone do that*? It simply makes no sense.

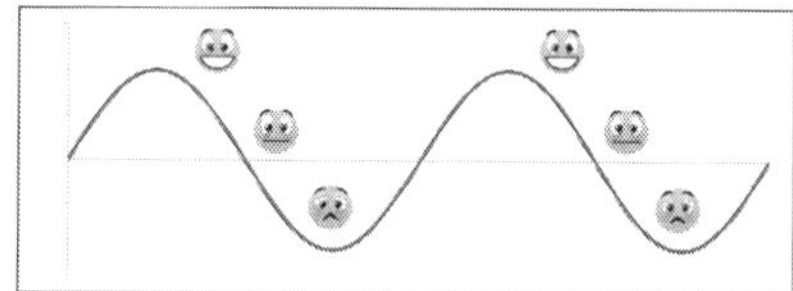

The Emotional Roller Coaster

My breakthrough came one evening while studying to speak at a youth retreat. I came across the following phrase: "Emotions are not good custodians of truth."

I could not have agreed more with that statement. The reality is that sometimes our emotions just do not tell us the truth. I had learned in Psychology 101 that emotions are unstable and unreliable when it comes to making decisions. A recent *Psychology Today*[20] article explained that feelings are not facts and sometimes our feelings are difficult to understand and even trust. I also read in Scripture that God would never leave me nor forsake me (see Deuteronomy 31:6). Evidently, I reasoned, whether we sense this feeling or not, He is there. We must determine to believe and walk by faith.

Many things produce an emotional response. Some are in the moment, others are from our past, and many people get destabilized worrying about the uncertain future. Still other emotions may be a response to mere fantasies, lies we tell ourselves that make us needlessly unhappy. They may also be a result of misunderstandings. A few feelings simply come from something we ate. There is no end to the amount of feeling, both positive and negative, that flows through our lives on a daily basis.

20 Psychology Today, Feelings are Not Facts, August 3, 2015.

The trick is to learn how to differentiate between feelings that are born out of our imagination and those that are real and verifiable, feelings that are substantive and can be trusted and feelings that deceive us. How then is this done?

Psychology calls this the battle for control between the elephant brain and the CEO part of our brain. The elephant brain is primal and jumps to conclusions. The CEO part of our brain is more rational and logical. You must decide which of these brains you're going to allow to control your life.

James also presents a situation like this, describing a person who is "like a ship tossed to and fro on the waves of the sea . . . double minded in all their ways" (James 1:6-7). According to James, the opposite of this is being "mature and complete" (James 1:4) NIV.

I learned the only way to get off this emotional and/or spiritual roller coaster was to find a way to stabilize my life. I had to stop the extreme ups and downs and find a way to level out my thoughts and feelings. The remedy came another evening while I was reading Scripture. I was studying the term *grace* for a Systematic Theology class when I had a wonderful epiphany: "For it is by grace you have been saved, through faith—and this is not from yourselves, it is the gift of God" (Ephesians 2:8, *NIV*).

I immediately started looking up all the passages that talked about the *grace of God*. It was as if God was shouting through the windows of my soul, "I believe in you! There is nothing you can do that will ever cause Me to leave you or forsake you." I learned through this desert experience that we all have a "grace story." Just listen to the words of Paul:

> Therefore, since we have been justified through faith, we have *peace* with God through our Lord Jesus Christ, through whom we have gained access by faith into this grace in which we now stand. And we boast in the *hope* of the glory of God. Not only so, but we also glory in our sufferings, because we know that suffering produces perseverance; perseverance, character; and character, HOPE. And hope does not put us to shame . . . (Romans 5:1-5, *NIV*).

> Let us then approach *God's throne of grace* with confidence, so that we may receive mercy and find grace to help us in our time of need (Hebrews 4:16, *NIV*).

Pastor Tom Sterbens explains this *grace* phenomenon as a miraculous "push back" against all things that would seek to consume and destroy us. Pastor Tom believes that wherever we read of *grace* in the New Testament, we are reading of the force of God resisting the otherwise predictable outcome of the presence and force of sin.

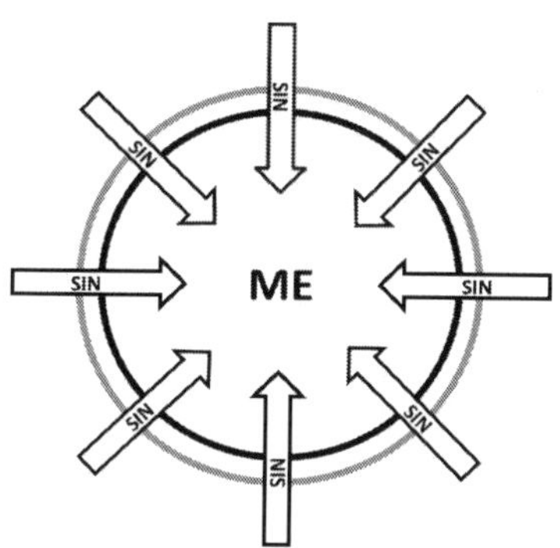

"Where sin did abound . . ."

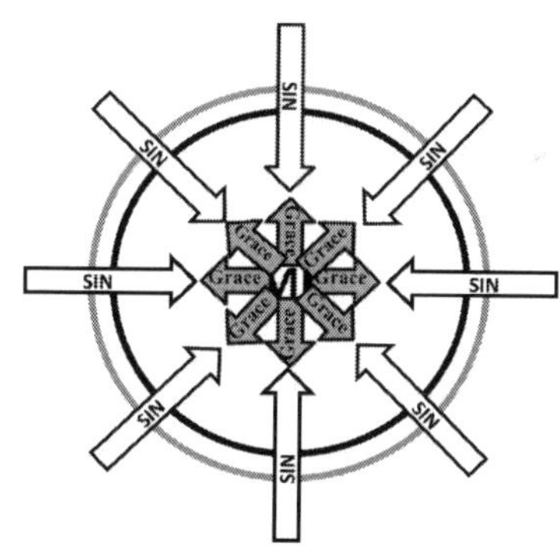

"Grace . . ."

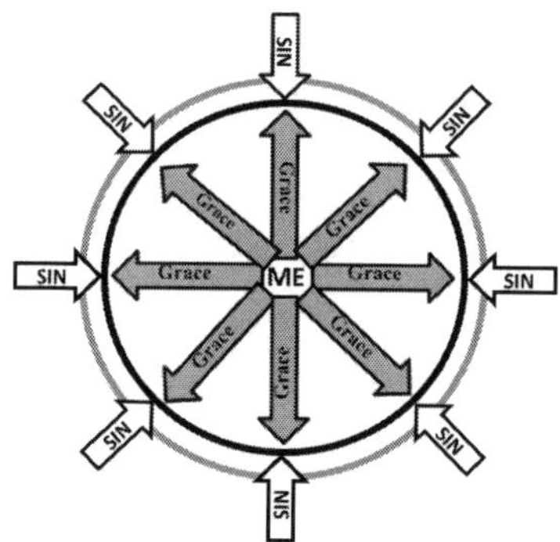

"Did much more abound."

Another important lesson came out of this experience with *grace*: *Your faith journey is not over when you fall. It's over when you stop getting up.*

Where would any of us be without the unmerited grace of God? It took *grace* to get me off that roller coaster.

Interestingly, my new life as a Christian immediately plunged me into personal development, a concept I would later come to understand as discipleship. I instantaneously became captivated with the Bible and the Gospel or Good News about the kingdom of God. For me, what Jesus taught was naturally connected to the idea of discipleship and personal change. But for many in Christian culture today, anything more than forgiveness of sins (the promise of heaven when you die) is optional. It does seem to me, however, that one (forgiveness) without the other (discipleship and personal change) is an incomplete version of what Jesus taught and, furthermore, leaves us unequipped for life now.

In this regard Dallas Willard[21] questioned, "If you don't die tonight, what are you going to do tomorrow?" The answer should be, 'I'm going to live a Christian life that makes a difference in this world. A life that proclaims the Good News of hope to my world." So the real issue in life is when we're not in church—what are you going to do?

If you do die tonight you may go to Heaven, but you see most people are not going to die tonight. They, like the rest of us, have to face life tomorrow and the day after and the day after.

"The big question is, 'Are you going to live life on your own tomorrow and the day after?' and if you do then you're not trusting Jesus.

According to Dallas Willard,

> Many people treat the time before you die as if somehow it had nothing to do with God. God has nothing to do with your life here, we're just hanging on, trying not to sin and we all fail and we have a whole teaching that you never make any progress, and that you don't have to make any progress, because you're saved by Grace. Grace, to them, relates only to forgiveness; it doesn't relate to life.

Grace does apply to forgiveness, but grace is much more than that. The general idea that fits all the contexts of grace found in the both the Old and

21 Dallas Willard was a professor, prolific writer, and thought leader. He passed away in 2016.

the New Testaments is this: Grace is God acting in my life to accomplish what I cannot accomplish on my own.

This could be why the Apostle Paul said, "I am not sufficient as to think anything of myself. My sufficiency is of God" (2 Corinthians 3:5, *paraphrased*).

"And we know that God causes everything to work together for the good of those who love God and are called according to his purpose for them."

(Romans 8:28, *NLT*)

CHAPTER 16

Beginning With the End in Mind

I made it through another full year at Lee College and headed home once more for summer break. I understood full well that I had a very big decision ahead of me, and I contemplated what I would do the entire ride home. Daddy was sick. His emphysema was getting worse, and he was not doing well at all. I was glad that summer break had come because it was providing me the opportunity to be with him. *But what would I do come September when college break was over? Would I leave my daddy again? Or would I make the decision to stay home and take care of him?* As it turned out, my decision wasn't difficult at all. I would miss my friends at college, but the decision to stay home was made even before I got to that old dirt road and the driveway of our mobile home.

I went to work again for the summer with my brother J.F. as a laborer on his brick crew. When summer was over, I decided to continue my college education by attending East Coast Bible College (ECBC), 30 miles south in Charlotte. I attended school during the day and worked as the janitor of my home church (Elm Street) in the afternoons and evenings. Pastor Don Anderson liked having me around, so he said. But I really knew all along that he was actually giving me a helping hand and keeping me on track.

Another semester of studies went by, and I was beginning to show some promise in relation to academics. During Christmas break, I really missed Lee College, but taking care of Daddy was much more important. I really enjoyed being at home with him, and we were doing things together we had never before done—for example, sitting together and watching TV. It's crazy how we take for granted people like our parents while growing up. They are our unconscious safety nets, always there in the back of our minds. I know I didn't consider my daddy as much as I should have, but I tried hard to make up for lost time.

Daddy got his Social Security check like clockwork the third day of every month. It wasn't much, but he looked forward to getting it. So every third of the month I'd plan to be off work and school to take him to the bank, to get Uncle William, and to go to Morrison's cafeteria at the local mall. That day was *their* day. Daddy loved that cafeteria, and it was the only time during the month that he'd get out. I was the designated driver.

Loss of My Safety Net

That Christmas would be my last holiday season with my daddy. He had been getting worse day by day, but that December he went downhill fast. The new year (1978) came in, and I stayed with Daddy basically around the clock. My sister JoAnn still had her drapery business in Charlotte, so she needed to be gone every day. My sister Patsy and her husband, Lee Roy, had recently moved up the road from us, so that brought some much-needed companionship and assistance. There wasn't anything the doctors could do except give Daddy pain medicine, so we tried to keep him as comfortable at home as possible.

It was Saturday night. We had made him comfortable on the living room couch so he could be around us all. I stayed up late with Daddy that night. I remember one simple conversation I had with him. "Daddy, you know I love you?" His reply, "Yes Freddie. And I love you too." I then said, "Daddy, it's important that you know you're ready to go to heaven. Are you ready?" "Yes, Freddie. I believe I'm ready," he replied. A few minutes later he fell asleep.

I went to bed in my little 6′ by 8′ bedroom located around the corner from the kitchen in our single-wide mobile home. I must have been exhausted because I don't remember anything until around daylight. Light coming through the rollout aluminum window of my tiny room woke me. I rolled over because I thought I heard Daddy come around the corner to my bedroom door. I'd heard him do that very thing thousands of times every morning, trying to get me out of bed for school. But as I opened my eyes to look, no one was there.

It couldn't have been 15-20 seconds when my sister JoAnn came around that corner and looked into my room, crying. "Freddie, Daddy just died."

I still believe to this day that as my daddy was on his way out of this world, he took time to come around that corner and check on me one final time. It was Sunday, January 8, 1978.

A couple of days later on Tuesday, January 10, we had Daddy's funeral at a funeral home in Charlotte and buried him beside my mama. Many of the family members came back to my house for dinner and fellowship. Most of them lingered way into the evening. Having everyone around helped considerably with the grief and strangeness that comes when you lose a family member. I had held it together fairly well until the funeral, and there I lost it. I could not believe Daddy was gone.

Daddy had not been a rich man. He never was able to provide much for me. But even during those times of alcoholism and grieving nights alone with him, I never doubted his love. I knew he was hurting and that was the only way he knew to get through it. And we got through it together.

A Few Fond Memories

We never went on vacations or to special places, ever. I remember Daddy sitting on a five-gallon bucket as he explained to me how to till the garden; watching him clean the catfish I caught the night before and fry them in an iron skillet; coming home late at night, knocking on the front door and hearing him walk through the living room to let me in, never complaining once; letting me drive his Ford Maverick as if it was mine. The only thing I ever remember my daddy fussing about was me running the gas out of his car. Morrison's cafeteria and trips to the bank or trips to visit a family member—this was as extravagant as it got. But he provided a safety net of love and security that helped me all the way through my life, especially from the time Mama died until we buried him. And now my safety net was gone.

It was approximately 11 p.m. on the day we buried Daddy. Everyone was gone except my sisters Patsy and JoAnn. We were sitting around our little kitchen table in our mobile home. I stood up and said, "Girls, there's really no reason for me to hang around here anymore. I believe I'll head back to Lee College."

I pulled together what few things I had, threw them into my '66 Plymouth, and pulled away from home once more. I was empty inside, grieving deeply, feeling very much alone. It was 12:15 a.m.

I cried for most of the next four and a half hours. I made it across Black Mountain on Interstate 40 and began to get sleepy. It was nearing 5a.m., and I could tell the sun was beginning to come up behind me. I came to a rest area just as I came through the winding mountain roadway between Asheville, North Carolina, and Knoxville, Tennessee. I pulled into the rest area, parked the car, and fell fast asleep.

Learning to Live Without Daddy

January 1978 started another semester at Lee College and the conscious struggle to live knowing that my unconscious safety net (Daddy) was no longer there. I did have help at this time during my life because I was able to live off campus. I moved into a large apartment with several college friends—Jimmy Lunsford, Kim Stone, and Roger Armstrong.

We were all members of an unsanctioned fraternity called the Dirty Half Dozen, or DHD for short. Dr. Bill George was the unofficial faculty sponsor. One of Dr. George's many talents was writing. Bill could turn a phrase better than anyone I ever personally knew. He also wrote many books and was a ghost writer[22] for many people. Dr. George actually dedicated one of his books to this motley group of young men in which he had tremendous faith. The dedication simply said:

To the Dirty Half Dozen
Who never really were dirty
And who now number many more than a half-dozen.

This particular semester at college moved along quickly. My biggest achievement was learning to become a better student and learning to actually *enjoy* learning. I spent every available evening moment when I wasn't working in the library. Library time became something I looked forward to.

That semester passed, and summer break came again. What was I going to do? Where was I going to go? My sister JoAnn still lived in the same single-wide mobile home I had called home, but Daddy was gone and it just no longer felt like "home." Pastor Don Anderson was now the superintendent of the Church of God Home for Children in Kannapolis. He invited me to live the summer in their newly created halfway house for

22 Ghost Writer—A person whose job it is to write material for someone else who is the named author.

college kids just like me. I appreciated the gesture, but that didn't seem to be the right thing to do either.

Somehow Dr. Bill George heard about my dilemma. He contacted me and offered to let me come live with him, his wife, Nelda, and his two young sons, Mike and David. An added advantage of this option was that I could also take a necessary internship of six credit hours during this same summer break. I accepted the offer and lived with the Georges for three full months, acting also as youth pastor for the church. I was only at the Dauphin Island Church for the summer, but the relationships I established with that youth group lasted for years. Some are still active to this day.

Bill George took advantage of this three-month period to pour as much into me as he possibly could. He was extremely intentional about my ministerial and personal development. I had to keep my first daily journal during that time, and Bill made sure I understood the benefits of journaling and reflection. Every week we visited, or I sat in on, some type of event or official occasion; *e.g.*, a wedding, a funeral, a dedication, a church service, a pastoral house call, a counseling session, or a hospital visit. The people involved with many of these events were completely unknown to us. Bill simply chose them to create dialogue and help me to learn right and wrong ways of doing things. It was challenging, inspiring, educational, and humbling.

My summer living with the Georges ended with Bill and Nelda taking me to Dallas, Texas, and my first Church of God General Assembly.[23] The road trip from Mobile to Dallas with the Georges, seeing a large meeting like that in a city like Dallas, and witnessing first-hand the decorum and structure involved was a great experience. When we returned from the Assembly, I packed up my '66 Plymouth and headed back to Lee College, thankful for the three months' development course I had just experienced.

---

23 The Church of God, with headquarters in Cleveland, Tennessee, United States, is a Pentecostal Christian denomination. With over six million members in over 180 countries, it is one of the largest Pentecostal denominations in the world. In the United States, it reports over one million members, making it one of the nation's largest denominations. The movement's origins can be traced back to 1886 with a small meeting of Christians at the Barney Creek Meeting House on the Tennessee/North Carolina border, making it the oldest Pentecostal denomination in the United States. The Church of God convenes a biennial assembly where all ministers and members attend to do the business of the church and to elect its leadership.

I arrived at Lee more determined than ever to become an even better student. I got my old jobs back, created a new schedule that fit everything in, and got to work. During this season of my life, I experienced a tremendous new feeling of confidence and hope. I even began to earn a fairly good amount of money. I decided to join with another DHD buddy and move into the Marquis Apartments. These apartments were rather upscale for a college student, but John Dawsey and I believed we could handle it, and so we did.

Situational Leadership would refer to this season of my life as Developmental Level 3 (D3), Capable but Cautious. Within this stage, the learner is consciously competent but still lacks confidence. D3 involves the continual development of skills and knowledge. Self-reliance is also emerging.

Situational Leadership 4 DEVELOPMENT LEVELS	
D4	High Competence High Commitment Inspired Inspires others
D3	High Competence Variable Commitment Not always confident, self-critical; may need help to look at things objectively.
D2	Some Competence Low Commitment Frustrated, Discouraged, overwhelmed, confused. Needs reassurance that mistakes are part of learning.
D1	Low Competence High Commitment Eager to learn, excited, Confidence based on hopes, not skills & not reality.

My work at the Cleveland Cosmopolitan Spa connected me to another professor who taught at Lee and who was also an entrepreneur, Dr. Roland Vines. Dr. Vines was attempting to catch the crest of the wave in the spa business in vogue at the time. He had just opened a spa in Jasper, Alabama. He found out during a Beech Mountain ski trip, sponsored by Lee College and chaperoned by Dr. Vines, that I worked at a spa and was their top membership salesperson.

We talked for weeks during the second semester of that year (1979) about the opportunity for me to manage his spa and train his people during the upcoming summer break. This would be a great opportunity for me, but it bothered me somewhat because I always felt my focus was to be on ministry and not on the corporate world and making money. I needed money, however, to pay for my college tuition, so this seemed like an answer to prayer.

Eeny, Meeny, Miny, Moe

As another college year ended, I found myself loading up that '66 Plymouth and taking off to Jasper, Alabama. Dr. Vines allowed several of us working at the spa to live at a lakehouse he owned. Nice! I continued, however, to be plagued by the thought that I should be doing ministry, not business. Adding insult to injury was the fact that a pastor from Oak Ridge, Tennessee, Pastor James Bandy, had offered me a summer job as their youth pastor. The opportunity, if it went well, also involved continuing to be their youth pastor during my entire senior year at college. They were going to allow me to drive up on weekends. I had chosen the larger paycheck over the ministry prospect.

I had been working for over a month at the spa, and all was going well. In fact, things were much better than well. I was making a lot of money, based mostly on commission sales of memberships and the people I was training. Making a lot of money and spending time on the lake water skiing was the life. What could be better?

I remember the day well. I was sitting in the living room of the lakehouse when the phone rang. Pastor James Bandy from the Oak Ridge Church had hunted me down and explained that he could not get me off his mind or out of his heart. He wanted to make one last attempt to get me to reconsider before moving on to consider other potential candidates for the youth minister position. I quickly explained that I believed I had made the right decision but appreciated his call. I hung up the phone and went water skiing with friends.

I had only been skiing a few minutes when the impression hit me like a ton of bricks. A sick feeling in my gut was telling me I had made the wrong choice. The impression was so impactful that I stopped skiing, ran immediately soaking wet into the house, and called Pastor Bandy. I explained I had changed my mind and that if he'd have me, I'd be there that coming Sunday. He hired me. It was Wednesday afternoon.

I spoke that evening at a nearby church in Sumiton, Alabama. A member of the church who was present that evening happened to be a car dealer. He came to me after the service and told me he felt impressed to help me. He noticed the old 1966 Plymouth I was driving and said a minister needed to be driving a more reliable automobile. I went down to his car lot the next morning, and when all was said and done, I had traded in my old reliable for a much newer 1976 Plymouth Cordova.

I had told Dr. Vines the night before, just after service, that I believed I had missed the boat with my decision to work the summer at the spa and that I believed I needed to be at the Oak Ridge Church. Dr. Vines laughed out loud. "Fred, I am surprised you lasted this long. I always suspected you would choose ministry over a job like this." He thanked me for helping get the spa off to a good start, gave me his blessing, and I was relieved.

By late that Thursday afternoon I was on the road, driving my new car and beginning to get excited about what was just around the bend on this journey of mine. I drove three hours to Cleveland, Tennessee, and spent a couple of days with friends, then drove the remaining 85 miles to Oak Ridge that Saturday afternoon. I felt at home when I pulled into town.

Oak Ridge, Tennessee

That first Sunday at Oak Ridge Church of God fit like a hand in a glove. I loved Pastors James and Betty Bandy. They made me feel like part of their family. They also surprised me with a little two-bedroom apartment just across a field from the church, definitely within walking distance. I thought I'd hit the lottery when he explained they were going to pay me $125 a week, plus my rent and utilities. I was in high cotton.

I worked that summer with the youth group as both the adult and youth departments started to grow. At the end of the summer break, Pastor Bandy told me they wanted me to stay on. I would need to drive up on Wednesdays for the midweek youth service and then drive back up on Fridays for the weekends, staying and speaking each Sunday evening. I knew this was going to be difficult, but I accepted and drove back and forth my entire senior year of college. And I loved every minute of it!

Graduation Day

My final year at Lee College flew by. I was so busy I didn't have time to think about how much I was doing. While at school, studying consumed my time. When in Oak Ridge, my young people consumed my time. Needless to say, I dropped all my other jobs and focused on school and ministry. I was honored to be tapped by

Alpha Gamma Chi (ATX), a fraternity on campus. I was also honored my senior year to be tapped as "Beau"[24] of Sigma Nu Sigma, a ladies sorority. I simply had no more time to give.

However, during this last year I decided to go after the darling of the Lee College campus. Shirley Jones was arguably the best-looking girl on campus and probably the best-looking girl in East Tennessee. How or why in the world *I* caught her eye and heart still mystifies me to this day, but it happened. I believe it all occurred one day after an intramural softball game. I saw her standing beside her Corvette Stingray (her daddy, Ted, was a car dealer), and I decided to do something crazy and bold—steal a kiss. She was parked on the side of the road beside the ballfield, and a huge crowd was gathered there watching the games. I walked over to her and asked for a kiss on the cheek. She closed her eyes and reached up to kiss my cheek. But I suddenly turned my head and her lips met mine. It blew her mind. I wish you could have seen her face—and the faces of all those standing around who saw it. I simply turned and confidently walked toward my car and home. To this day I believe there and then I put her heart in my pocket. Yes!

That May 1980 I became the first in my family to graduate from college. My first semester I earned a 1.7 GPA and remained on academic probation. I graduated with a 3.0 GPA and debt free. Two miracles! What's more, as you can now see, these were only a few miraculous occurrences that happened on my life journey to get me to graduation day.

24 Beau—A young man chosen by a ladies' sorority to be "best man on campus" to represent their values and principles.

Fred on Lee College Ski Trip with Marlon Rampy - 1979

Lee College DHD Softball Team 1978

Fred with his brother J.F. 1980

One of Fred's Paintings Lee College

Fred and Shirley Christmas 1981

SECTION FOUR

The rest of the story.

CHAPTER 17

The Rest of My Story

Paul Harvey was an American radio broadcaster for the ABC radio network from the 1950s to the 1990s. He was famous for providing the news in a novel, interesting, and relevant manner. He was also famous for giving the news in two parts, what he called "page one" and "the rest of the story." What I have provided thus far in terms of my life journey represents "page one." The remainder of my journey will be told in part two, "the rest of the story."

Page one, regarding the first half of my story, involved a narrative filled with loss and pain, until that fork in the road in January 1974. The day I made the choice to become a Christian truly was a bifurcation point, a divergence. It was the day I decided to separate myself from the past and walk in a new direction. From that day forward, many things in my life were altered and the dark cloud that had covered me seemed to have been blown away. That dark cloud was replaced with what Shirley has called during our entire life together "the happy cloud." It's true. I have lived under the happy cloud. Good things just seemed to happen to me, to us. Even the terrible things meant for harm turned around for good. I'm not saying there was never any more pain or heartache. In fact, over the next half of my life and as of the writing of this book, I lost these special people:

- My pastor and surrogate father Don Anderson
- My brother Jimmy
- My sister JoAnn
- My sister Virginia

- My best friend Bobby Kiser
- My other brother J.F.
- My friend and adopted sister Pam Adams
- My friend, encourager, and father-in-law Ted Jones
- My mentors and friends, Bob and Clara Pace.
- And my greatest counselor, adviser, and mentor Dr. Bill George.

I am no stranger to pain and loss, but optimism and goodness just seem to be the climate of our lives. Remember, I've said several times that no magic wands are waved over our heads. There are no magic bullets. No magic words or phrases can instantly make us optimistic, content, or happy. *To be happy is a choice we make.*

> And God is able to bless you abundantly, so that in all things at all times, having all that you need, you will abound in every good work (2 Corinthians 9:8, *NIV*).
>
> And we know that God causes everything to work together for the good of those who love God and are called according to his purpose for them (Romans 8:28, *NLT*).

Fred with his sister, Patsy, and brother, J.F.
1994

Fred and Shirley's Wedding Shower, May 1982
with Shirley's parents, Claudia and Ted Jones

Fred's PhD Graduation Reception, July 2003
Shirley, Fred, and Dr. Bill George

Snap Shots of Life

CHAPTER 18

Page Two

Allow me to provide a preview, a few clips of what's to come by giving kind of a bullet-point glance at where my life has taken me.

From Lee University to Oak Ridge, Tennessee

I worked for the Oak Ridge Church of God for three years following graduation from Lee College in May 1980.

I'll never forget standing in my sister JoAnn's drapery shop when she said, "Freddie, I believe Shirley is your Rachael." JoAnn was, of course, referring to the biblical love story regarding Jacob and Rachael (see Genesis 29). She was encouraging me and giving me her blessing.

Shirley graduated a year before me in 1979 with a business degree. We started dating officially my senior year at Lee and continued dating for several years following my graduation. On May 25, 1982, we married. As of the writing of this book, we have been married for 36 years. She has been my partner and has literally co-authored my life.

Shirley's natural gifting with numbers, and her experience in her dad's car business, have served us well through the years that followed. Even though Shirley did not grow up in the Church of God, her parents did bring her up in church. Her Kentucky conservative upbringing helped us navigate many cultural landmines and blind spots.

Oak Ridge, Tennessee, to Apple Valley, Minnesota

We left Oak Ridge and pastored for a short time in Apple Valley, Minnesota. We were newly married and lived 1,200 miles from family or friends. We were also both relative novices to the work of ministry. I served in a dual role while in Minnesota—as the state youth director and pastor of the Apple Valley Church of God.

Minnesota to Corbin, Kentucky

We left Minnesota and moved to Corbin, Kentucky, Shirley's hometown. I actually worked for a while in a grocery store that Shirley's brother, Mike, and I partnered to start. But I never was meant for something like that. Shirley's dad, Ted, knew this to be true as well. Ted helped us purchase a motorhome, and we took another step of faith by traveling around the country and preaching revival meetings. This really was a much bigger miracle than anyone will ever know because neither Shirley nor I had grown up in the Church of God. Getting opportunities to speak was difficult. We were, however, industrious and energetic and were actually rather successful.

Corbin, Kentucky, to a Motorhome

Shirley and I traveled from state to state, town to town, speaking in different churches. We were with Pastor Bill and Nelda George in Mobile, Alabama, when we received a call from Pastor T.L. Lowery. We had spoken for Pastor Lowery earlier in the year and now he was inquiring if we'd be interested in moving to Washington, D.C., to be youth pastor at his church. The opportunity could not have been more fortuitous and yet miraculous because we had just learned one day earlier that we were expecting our first child.

A Motorhome to Washington, D.C.

We accepted that opportunity and worked in Washington, D.C., with Dr. T.L. Lowery as youth pastors for two years. We loved our work there, the friends we made, especially those on staff, and we spent most every day off touring downtown D.C. Our first daughter, Marissa Anne, was born just outside the Beltway in Fort Washington, Maryland.

Washington, D.C., Back to Cleveland, Tennessee

We went from Washington, D.C., back to Cleveland, Tennessee, to be youth pastors at North Cleveland Church of God. We served the North Cleveland Church for two wonderful years.

Cleveland to Lake City, Florida

We then left Cleveland again to be senior pastor of our second church, this time in Lake City, Florida. Our second daughter, Whitney Autumn, was born in Gainesville, Florida, while we were pastoring in Lake City. While there we bought 12 and a half acres of land located right on Interstate 75, and, with the assistance of Men and Women of Action (MWOA), a construction and humanitarian arm of the Church of God, physically built a 10,000-square-foot church from the ground up.

Lake City, Florida, to Lehigh Acres, Florida

Our next move took us further south to Lehigh Acres, Florida. Lehigh was located just outside Fort Myers, Florida, on the Gulf Coast. We spent the next nine years pastoring in Lehigh. I loved Southwest Florida, and we watched our two girls grow up while in that area. While pastoring in Lehigh Acres, I was chosen "Clergy Person of the Year" in the *Southwest Florida Newspress.*

The Benefits of Physical Exercise

I loved playing basketball and became fairly good as time passed. In fact, playing basketball became a daily event on my calendar from noon till 1 p.m., Monday through Friday, for years. No matter where I lived, I found a lunchtime group that met to play basketball—in Cleveland, Oak Ridge, and Lehigh Acres. I guess it was the jumping, but eventually my knees would no longer take the pounding.

Therefore, I decided while living in Southeast Florida to try jogging, and I loved it! Three-mile running events (5Ks) gave way to six-mile events (10Ks). I vividly remember how exhilarating it was the evening I stayed on my feet, running for more than 60 minutes. It was awesome! But that distance and achievement moved aside for a greater goal—the half-marathon (13.1 miles). And that led to a full marathon (26.2 miles). To date, I've completed more than 40 half-

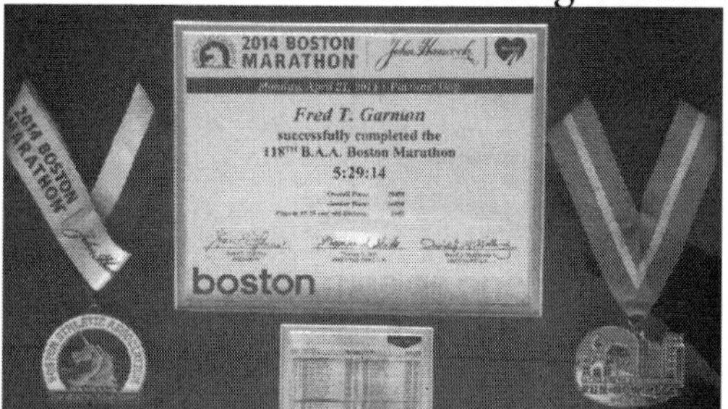

marathons and two full marathons. I hope there are many more such events in these legs of mine.

Running for me has something to do with setting goals, both short-term and long-term, and achieving them. In addition, several outcomes make jogging extremely beneficial. First, it keeps your weight down. Second, jogging releases wonderful attitude-enhancing endorphins. And the fact that jogging releases endorphins that literally help maintain stress and a positive attitude is exponentially added value! Third, it helps to structure your life. This byproduct that comes with a consistent regimen of jogging I call "ordering your private world." I found that whenever I maintained a regular and structured physical routine, it almost by default helped me maintain a more structured life. Conversely, whenever I slacked in my physical activity, I also started to get unorganized in other areas of my life.

Lehigh Acres back to Oak Ridge

We were called back to Oak Ridge, Tennessee, to serve once again at the Oak Ridge Church of God—this time, 17 years later, as senior pastor. Pastor Bandy was retiring after 33 years, and the church board asked us to return. During our tenure at Oak Ridge, I was honored as "Clergy Person of the Year" in Oak Ridge and the East Tennessee Region. I was also honored to serve as an Olympic Torch Bearer for the 2002 Olympics held in Salt Lake City. The honor was bestowed in recognition of outstanding community service.

We spent the next 10 years pastoring in Oak Ridge. During this time I committed three years to pursuing my master of divinity (M.Div.) degree from the Church of God Theological Seminary (now Pentecostal Theological Seminary). Then I jumped immediately into a doctoral program at Regent University where I subsequently earned my Doctor of Philosophy (PhD) degree in Organizational Leadership. It was the hardest thing, hands down, I ever did in my life. And I could have never accomplished it without the help of my wife, Shirley, and our music director at the time, Phil Thompson. Phil is still a best friend to this day.

It took me three years to complete my PhD, and I was employed by Regent University's Doctor of Strategic Leadership program (DSL) to teach part-time as an adjunct professor prior to receiving my PhD. In fact, I was teaching at a residency for the DSL doctoral program when I defended[25] my PhD dissertation. The faculty requested that I defend while on campus and that I allow all residency students and available professors to sit in on and observe my defense. I agreed and later on wondered why I would willfully add such pressure to an already pressurized event. Scores of students and professors crowded the regal lecture hall on campus that day to watch my defense. My topic of defense was "conflict in leadership" and specifically focused on "conflict in ministry leadership." I can still vividly remember the moment, about 45 minutes into my presentation and defense time, that I felt the mood of the defense move from one of inquiry to one of collegial discussion. It was also at that time that my dissertation chair professor opened the defense for general audience discussion. It was a most rewarding experience.

After a considerable time of open dialogue, I was, along with everyone in the room, asked to leave the dissertation committee alone to deliberate. They were to discuss whether or not I had passed or failed. Everyone—and I mean everyone—stood in the hallway with me waiting. Then the huge doors opened. My dissertation committee stood together in the doorway and said together, "Dr. Garmon, you passed." It was a moment of tremendous pride and accomplishment. How could a nobody named Ordinary, from the Land of Familiar, have ever gotten to this place? And to think ... it all started with a *kernel of hope*. I guess I *was* lucky number eight.

While getting my PhD, Shirley and I decided to start a leadership nonprofit. For what, we weren't sure, but we knew that one of the eventualities of our future involved leadership training and development for others. I loved leadership training and was passionate about sharing

25 A *dissertation* is a document submitted in support of candidature for an academic degree presenting the author's research and findings. The term "dissertation" is normally applied to a doctorate. The required complexity or quality of research of a dissertation can vary by country, university, or program, and the required minimum study period may thus vary significantly in duration. My program involved two years book work and research followed by comprehensive exams, and if passed the candidate is given up to five years to complete the dissertation project. I was able to complete the entire program in under three years. It required extreme focus and concentration.

everything I had learned. I was putting everything I learned into practice in terms of real-life leadership. We called our new fledgling enterprise "LeaderLABS" and sought and received nonprofit status from the government. Even though I developed and taught leadership all over the world during the next 11 years, it was some time before we officially formalized and began to use LeaderLABS as a ministry.

A few years after earning my PhD, I got the opportunity to serve as director of a humanitarian organization called People for Care and Learning (PCL). PCL served primarily in the Southeast Asia country of Cambodia. This move was another one of those steps of faith where you again take a deep breath and step out into the unknown. Shirley and I had spent our lives building our ministry to a place of relevant financial security. We had a church of approximately 900 members (1,000-plus attendance at Easter and Christmas productions). And we loved Oak Ridge and the East Tennessee foothills of the Smokey Mountains. With some trepidation and responsible concern, I accepted the directorship of PCL, especially after the Board of Directors explained they had good news and bad news. The good news was that they would set my salary to equal that which I was presently getting at the church. The bad news was that PCL didn't have any money and that I had to raise all operational and program funds, along with my salary. It was another step of faith. But with a deep breath, Shirley and I stepped out. And did I mention both daughters were in college at the time?

I spent the next 11 years traveling back and forth from Cambodia 53 times and traveling all over the USA raising literally millions of dollars for that poverty-stricken country. In the process, our work with the poor got the attention of the Cambodian government, and we partnered together on several major projects. The biggest was the "Build A City" project where we literally built a city for thousands of poverty-stricken families living in the refugee village of Andong, just outside Phnom Penh, Cambodia. The Cambodian government honored me and PCL with several humanitarian medals of humanitarian nobility and also gave the Church of God official status in the Kingdom of Cambodia with full rights to own property and plant churches.

Humanitarian Honor at "Build A City" Dedication

It was during this season that the Church of God also honored me by requesting that I serve as superintendent of Southeast Asia, overseeing the countries of Cambodia, Vietnam, Thailand, Myanmar, Laos, and Sri Lanka. With these countries being on the complete opposite side of the world, it did not take long to become a "Million Miler" with Delta Airlines.

I stepped away from being superintendent of Southeast Asia in July 2016 after serving five years in that position and also stepped down from leading PCL on December 31, 2016. I did this because I wanted to continue following my passion and my big dream—to train leaders. During this next season of my life, I plan to train leaders using an Executive Leadership program I have created called "The Ten Essential Skills of Executive Leadership" (*www.leaderlabs.com*).

Preparing for an Eventuality

According to the Chinese sage Confucius, if you love what you do, you'll never work a day in your life. I have found this statement partially true. As you have seen in these pages, there was a season of my life where I did many laboring jobs that I did not necessarily "love." Each one, however, represented a necessary means to an end (agency). Life goes to another level entirely when a person can connect their purpose and their passion with their vocation. As Dr. Bruce Winston put it during my first day of PhD residency in Virginia Beach, Virginia, "You don't know it or understand it now. But you're preparing for an eventuality you don't know is going to happen."

No statement could have ever been more true or prophetic. In fact, I believe that statement provides definition for each and every step of my journey since that third Sunday in January 1974 when "lucky number eight" made the decision to kneel at that altar.

I have found that clarity is perhaps the most important concept a person needs in his/her personal toolbelt. You must decide what you want to achieve in each area of your life, be absolutely clear about your goals and objectives, and then don't deviate from them. In doing this one thing, you will be stepping on the accelerator of your personal potential.

James said in James 6:1-8 some important words concerning clarity:

. . . You must believe and not doubt, because the one who doubts is like a wave of the sea, blown and tossed by the wind. That person should not expect to receive anything from the Lord. Such a person is double-minded and unstable in all they do (James 6:1-8, *NIV*).

Napoleon Hill, American writer, seems to agree completely: "There is one quality which one must possess to win, and that is definiteness of purpose, the knowledge of what one wants, and a burning desire to achieve it."

I hope you've seen by now that the title of this book, *Lucky Number 8*, is simply a play on words. I was the last of eight children in my family, but luck had nothing to do with the journey of my life. It had everything to do with *choices* that allowed *grace*, *hope*, and *favor* to take seed in my life.

In fact, graphs depicting historical data shows that families of eight

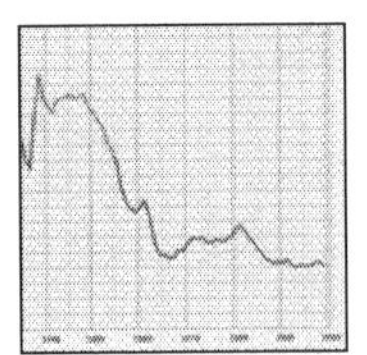

to 10 children dove around 1960, just three years after I was born in 1957. Families like mine with eight or more children were much more likely back in the first half of the 1900s. Birth control was introduced in 1960, abortion on demand in 1973,[26] and the unprecedented participation of women in the workforce increased.

26 Roe v. Wade, 410 U.S. 113 (1973), is a landmark decision by the United States Supreme Court on the issue of abortion.

In 1900 America was a nation of 76 million people, nearly 31 million of whom were children under 18. A baby born in 1900 was expected to live only to the age of 49. By 1958, our population had increased two and a quarter times to a total of 174 million.

The exact beginning and end of the baby boom can be debated. In the United States, demographers usually use mid-1946 to mid-1964. Most baby boomers are now in their 60s or 70s, with the oldest boomer 76 years old. I am presently 60. And now, according to the U.S. Census report, the American family has declined to its smallest size on record.

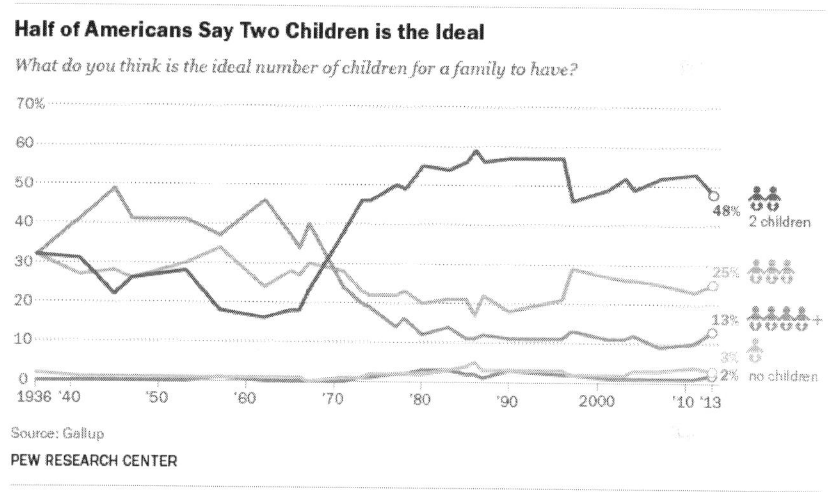

Pew Research Center - Two Children per Family

In today's culture, a family with eight children is worthy of a reality television series. For example, on April 4, 2007, *Jon & Kate Plus 8* aired on national television. During its run, the series was one of network TV's highest-rated programs, with the fifth-season premiere seen by a record 9.8 million viewers, the most-watched show of that evening, including broadcast television.

Hopefully you can understand *Lucky Number 8* definitely has meaning to me. I can't help but wonder if possibly the happy cloud concept of grace and favor didn't touch me while in my mother's womb. Otherwise. there were simply too many things against me. The stars were not aligned in my favor. It seemed I truly was "sabotaged to fail."

You cannot teach a person anything.
You can only help them find it
Within themselves.

—Galileo

CHAPTER 19

The Journey of a Thousand Miles

If the journey of a thousand miles begins with one step, my journey began a little earlier—when my two knees bowed that day in January 1974 to pray. I found out that all improvements in your outer life will begin with improvements on the inside. Galileo made a great point:

"You cannot teach a person anything; you can only help them find it within themselves."

I believe the point of Galileo's statement involves personal initiative. I now do a great deal of training via my LeaderLabs enterprise. I do it because I believe it makes a difference, altering at times the very direction and aim of a person's life. Training is a pathway. But for it to become successful, training has to become education and preparation. This conceptual and actual transformation occurs on the inside of a person—sometimes consciously, occasionally unconsciously. This transformation is also referred to in psychology as having self-efficacy.[27] It is my belief that self-efficacy was ignited that Sunday in 1974 when that kernel of grace and hope were germinated in my life. This is one of the miracles of Christian faith.

In this regard, John Gardner, a celebrated Stanford University professor and leadership thought giant, arguably gave one of the most influential speeches in American history on November 10, 1990. The title of his speech was "Personal Renewal." His talk focused on the need for leaders who wish to make a difference and remain effective to commit themselves to continued learning and growth, a principle known as "lifelong learning."

27 Psychologist Albert Bandura has defined *self-efficacy* as one's belief in one's ability to succeed in specific situations or accomplish a task. One's sense of self-efficacy can play a major role in how one approaches goals, tasks, and challenges.

To become a lifelong or lifetime learner, a person must first become motivated toward further learning and confident in their ability to achieve transformational goals via self-directed learning. Two fundamental issues confront this idea of continued lifetime learning. First, too many people emerge from basic schooling without confidence in themselves as learners. Second, others who have had some measure of education and consequent success suffer from what Peter Drucker called "intellectual arrogance." They don't believe they need any additional education. I see this as part of my mission—to empower potential by way of *inspirational* leadership development programs. Christian nomenclature would say I'm a "leadership evangelist."

As Albert Einstein, German physicist, said, "Wisdom is not a product of schooling, but of a lifelong attempt to acquire it."

Knowledge Management

Today's learners are flooded with more information than we can handle. Tomorrow's learners will need to know far more than any one person can retain. Learning, therefore, can no longer be dichotomized into a place and time to acquire knowledge. Lifelong learning is no longer simply a possibility or luxury to be considered; it is an essential challenge for everyone. It is a mindset and a habit for people to acquire. We need to understand both self-directed learning and collaborative learning. We need each other.

Consequently, much of what I do today involves bringing people to a higher level of awareness.... Awareness that Christian belief brings with it the gift of hope and grace. Awareness that the kernel of hope, once germinated, inspires transformational potential. And awareness that lifelong learning is the key that unlocks the personal growth process. There is no magic wand or silver bullet, only impetus.

Addicted to Learning

It only took a kernel of *hope* to ignite a seed of *potential*. And I have learned that you can actually develop a "positive addiction" to learning. Learning produces enhanced clarity, confidence, and competence. When you tap into this addiction, you will at an unconscious level have the ability to lead and organize your life. You'll possess the ability to search for, find, and download into your brain every relevant piece of information in a "just-in-time" manner. Don't forget the story of the man who stopped a musician on the street in New York and asked how he could get to Carnegie Hall. The musician replied, "Practice, man, practice." Practice is the key to mastering any skill. Your mind is like a muscle. It grows stronger and more capable with use. With practice, you can learn any behavior or develop any habit you consider either desirable or necessary.

Leadership is really a story—a co-constructed story involving the essential ingredients of talent, skills, and experience bridged by context, perspective, and time. Even after all my learning and preparation concerning the subject of personal growth and leadership, I still find myself wondering what it takes to make someone a *great* leader. The adages, "Leaders are born, not made," or the opposite, "Leaders are made, not born," just leave me with more questions.

I choose to say, "Leaders are born, *then* made." Each of us is born, and each of us is presented with multiple choices in life. Choosing to tap into *hope*, and choosing to love learning, places one in a position of personal preparation. And personal preparation sets one in the place to be ready when the opportunity to lead presents itself.

I'm proud to say that I am still passionately learning, practicing, and preparing each and every day. I am anticipating the next adventure and the next unknown eventuality. And I remain excited about the journey.

Stay tuned for "the rest of the story." God's not finished with me yet.

And I am certain that God, who began the good work within you, will continue his work until it is finally finished . . . (Philippians 1:6, *NLT*).

Fred sitting on his "Back Porch."

APPENDIX 1

The Future "Hope" Scale

Directions:

Read each item carefully. Using the scale shown below, please *honestly* select the number that best describes *you* and put that number in the blank provided.

1. = Definitely False
2. = Mostly False
3. = Somewhat False
4. = Slightly False
5. = Slightly True
6. = Somewhat True
7. = Mostly True
8. = Definitely True

1. I can think of many ways to get out of a jam. ___
2. I energetically pursue my goals. ___
3. I feel tired most of the time. ___
4. There are lots of ways around any problem. ___
5. I am easily downed in an argument. ___
6. I can think of many ways to get the things in life that are important to me. ___
7. I worry about my health. ___
8. Even when others get discouraged, I know I can find a way to solve the problem. ___
9. My past experiences have prepared me well for my future. ___
10. I've been pretty successful in life. ___

11. I usually find myself worrying about something. ___

12. I meet the goals that I set for myself. ___

Scoring: Items 2, 9, 10, and 12 make up the agency subscale. ___

Items 1, 4, 6, and 8 make up the pathway subscale. ___

Agency Scale

Your "goal directed" energy.

1 2 3 4 5 6 7 8 9 10 11 12 13 14 15 ***16*** 17 18 19 20 21 22 23 24 25 26 27 28 29 30 31 32

Pathways Scale

Your drive to "plan and accomplish goals."

1 2 3 4 5 6 7 8 9 10 11 12 13 14 15 ***16*** 17 18 19 20 21 22 23 24 25 26 27 28 29 30 31 32

Description of the Hope Scale Measure:

A 12-item measure of a respondent's level of hope.

In particular, the scale is divided into two subscales that comprise Snyder's cognitive model of hope:

(1) Agency (*i.e.*, goal-directed energy)

(2) Pathways (*i.e.*, planning to accomplish goals).

Of the 12 items, four make up the Agency subscale and four make up the Pathways subscale.

The remaining four items are fillers.

*Findings indicate that hopelessness is a strong predictor of adverse health outcomes, independent of depression and traditional risk factors.

APPENDIX 2

Rokeach Values Survey

Terminal and Instrumental Values

On the following two pages are two lists of values, each in alphabetical order. Each value is accompanied by a short description and a blank space. Your goal is to rank each value in its order of importance to you for each of the two lists. Study each list and think of how much each value may act as a guiding principle in your life.

To begin, select the value that is of most importance to you. Write the number 1 in the blank space next to that value. Next, choose the value that is second in importance to you and write the number 2 in the blank next to it. Work your way through the list until you have ranked all 18 values on this page. The value that is of least importance to you should have the number 18.

When you have finished ranking all 18 values, turn the page and rank the next 18 values in the same way. Please do each page separately.

When ranking, take your time and think carefully. Feel free to go back and change your order should you have second thoughts about any of your answers. When you have completed the ranking of both sets of values listed on the following two pages, the result should represent an accurate picture of how you really feel about what's important in your life.

Terminal Values

A Comfortable Life ___
a prosperous life

Equality ___
brotherhood and equal opportunity for all

An Exciting Life ___
a stimulating, active life

Family Security ___
taking care of loved ones

Freedom ___
independence and free choice

Health ___
physical and mental well-being

Inner Harmony ___
freedom from inner conflict

Mature Love ___
sexual and spiritual intimacy

National Security ___
protection from attack

Pleasure ___
an enjoyable, leisurely life

Salvation ___
saved; eternal life

Self-Respect ___
self-esteem

A Sense of Accomplishment ___
a lasting contribution

Social Recognition ___
respect and admiration

True Friendship ___
close companionship

Wisdom ___
a mature understanding of life

A World at Peace ___
a world free of war and conflict

A World of Beauty ___
beauty of nature and the arts

Ambitious ___
hardworking and aspiring

Broad-minded ___
open-minded

Capable ___
competent; effective

Clean ___
neat and tidy

Courageous ___
standing up for your beliefs

Forgiving ___
willing to pardon others

Helpful ___
working for the welfare of others

Honest ___
sincere and truthful

Imaginative ___
daring and creative

Instrumental Values

Independent ___
self-reliant; self-sufficient

Intellectual ___
intelligent and reflective

Logical ___
consistent; rational

Loving ___
affectionate and tender

Loyal ___
faithful to friends or the group

Obedient ___
dutiful; respectful

Polite ___
courteous and well-mannered

Responsible ___
dependable and reliable

Self-controlled ___
restrained; self-disciplined